VOID

Library of
Davidson College

CHURCH AND PEACE

Edited by
Virgil Elizondo
and
Norbert Greinacher

English Language Editor
Marcus Lefébure

T. & T. CLARK LTD.
Edinburgh

THE SEABURY PRESS
New York

261.8
C5612

Copyright © 1983, by Stichting Concilium, T. & T. Clark Ltd. and The Seabury Press
Inc. All rights reserved. Nothing contained in this publication shall be multiplied and/or
made public by means of print, photographic print, microfilm, or in any other manner
without the previous written consent of the Stichting Concilium, Nijmegen (Holland),
T. & T. Clark Ltd., Edinburgh (Scotland) and The Seabury Press Inc., New York
(USA).

April 1983
T. & T. Clark Ltd., 36 George Street, Edinburgh EH2 2LQ
ISBN: 0 567 30044 7

The Seabury Press, 815 Second Avenue, New York, NY 10017
ISBN: 0 8164 2444 6

Library of Congress Catalog Card No.: 82 062757

Printed in Scotland by William Blackwood & Sons Ltd., Edinburgh

83-4777

Concilium: Monthly except July and August.
Subscriptions 1983: UK and Rest of the World £27·00, postage and handling included;
USA and Canada, all applications for subscriptions and enquiries about *Concilium*
should be addressed to The Seabury Press, 815 Second Avenue, New York, NY 10017,
USA.

CONCILIUM

Religion in the Eighties

CONCILIUM

Editorial Directors

Giuseppe Alberigo	Bologna	Italy
Gregory Baum	Toronto	Canada
Leonardo Boff	Petrópolis	Brazil
Antoine van den Boogaard	Nijmegen	The Netherlands
Paul Brand	Ankeveen	The Netherlands
Marie-Dominique Chenu OP	Paris	France
John Coleman SJ	Berkeley, Ca.	USA
Mary Collins OSB	Washington	USA
Yves Congar OP	Paris	France
Mariasusai Dhavamony SJ	Rome	Italy
Christian Duquoc OP	Lyon	France
Virgil Elizondo	San Antonio, Texas	USA
Casiano Floristán	Madrid	Spain
Claude Geffré OP	Paris	France
Norbert Greinacher	Tübingen	West Germany
Gustavo Gutiérrez	Lima	Peru
Peter Huizing SJ	Nijmegen	The Netherlands
Bas van Iersel SMM	Nijmegen	The Netherlands
Jean-Pierre Jossua OP	Paris	France
Hans Küng	Tübingen	West Germany
Nicholas Lash	Cambridge	Great Britain
René Laurentin	Paris	France
Johannes-Baptist Metz	Münster	West Germany
Dietmar Mieth	Düdingen	Switzerland
Jürgen Moltmann	Tübingen	West Germany
Roland Murphy OCarm	Durham, NC	USA
Jacques Pohier OP	Paris	France
David Power OMI	Washington, DC	USA
Karl Rahner SJ	Munich	West Germany
Luigi Sartori	Padua	Italy
Edward Schillebeeckx OP	Nijmegen	The Netherlands
Elisabeth Schüssler Fiorenza	Hyattsville, Ind.	USA
David Tracy	Chicago	USA
Knut Walf	Nijmegen	The Netherlands
Anton Weiler	Nijmegen	The Netherlands
John Zizioulas	Glasgow	Great Britain

Lay Specialist Advisers

José Luis Aranguren	Madrid/Santa Barbara, Ca.	Spain/USA
Luciano Caglioti	Rome	Italy
August Wilhelm von Eiff	Bonn	West Germany
Paulo Freire	Perdizes, São Paulo	Brazil
Harald Weinrich	Munich	West Germany

Concilium 164 (4/1983): Practical Theology

CONTENTS

Editorial: Thou shalt not kill

THE COMMAND is so clear, yet humanity has camouflaged killing others in so many ways that it can easily and in good conscience go on sacrificing the lives of others for the sake of our own comfort and security. Only when the privileged of the Western World have been threatened with their own annihilation through their own creation of nuclear armaments has the question of the massive killing of peoples emerged as an urgent problem. Self-interest? We hope it is much more.

We recoil at the thought of the Aztecs who openly practised human sacrifices for the sake of their nation. Yet we endorse and support our multiple contemporary forms of human sacrifice which continue to take place for our survival. At least the Aztecs were open and honest about the sacrifice of others. We starve to death 40,000 infants per day in the Third World (Houtart) but call it economic stability. We rob people of their natural resources but call it development and progress (Houtart). We furnish military aid to oppressive dictatorial regimes known for their brutality, tortures and on-going genocide of their native populations and call it aid to the allies of the West (D'Escoto). We manufacture nuclear armaments for the sole purpose of destroying life on a massive scale but we call it the work of peace (Jegen). We mobilise public support and vote for increased military budgets for 'national defence'—but just who and what are we really defending (Comblin)? We shamelessly disguise the destruction of life—part of the confusion of Babel—so that it may appear as civilised, humane, prudent and necessary for law and order to continue. We do not want to face that with the growth of civilisation there appears to be an equal explosion of violence at all levels of human society—personal, structural and technological (Peachey). So, in today's world, to be civilised is to be violent!

Yet when the exploited, subjugated, oppressed and dying masses of the world—the sacrificial victims of the industrial powers of the world—mobilise to defend life (Linskens and D'Escoto) we condemn it as unjust aggression and violence. The rich nations claim the absolute right to defend their self-interests as a divine imperative while they condemn the efforts of the poor who struggle to claim their own God-given rights of liberty and self-determination. Does the commandment 'Thou shall not kill' apply only to the defenceless and oppressed of the world?

'Render to Caesar the things that are Caesar's and to God the things that are God's'—how we have perverted the understanding of this text since Constantine! Can the Christian churches continue to live the lie that gradually crept into Christendom since Christians came into power and identified the cause of Jesus with that of their State (Jegen and Missala)? In practice, we have not made the Caesars—the Holy Roman Empire, Ferdinand and Isabella, Napoleon, Hitler, the Falklands/Malvinas, the United States of America . . . —to be our Gods? Have we not rendered to our Caesar what belongs to God alone—the unquestioned loyalty in our love of neighbour and of enemy even to the point of giving our life for others (Pérez Esquivel).

For the past 1500 years, the churches have become accustomed to privilege and prestige. They have found it impossible to even conceive of pacifism (Zahn). The churches have been united to the goals of the State in such an intimate way that they have become one flesh even when secondary separations have been maintained. Can the Church divide itself from its own flesh and reunite itself to the flesh of its Master as he continues to take up the cause of the victims of society? As the Master was condemned for being blasphemous and a rebel-rouser, are the contemporary churches ready to be charged of the same 'crimes' for the sake of saving and liberating truth? Are today's Christians ready to be apprehended, flogged, threatened and held in public scorn for living and proclaiming the forbidden truth of this world: peace (Pérez Equivel)? No easy task! Our church-going people are too accustomed to the common flesh of the States and the Church. They are used to seeing high-ranking church officials serve as the chief of military chaplains and well-decorated officers serving as honour guards for church functions. They have become accustomed to each other. It seems so proper that it does not appear that it could be otherwise. Yet, this illicit concubinage must be broken if the Church is to return to its one true spouse—Jesus, the one saviour of the world.

John Paul II spoke in Hiroshima about the future of life on this planet as dependent 'upon one single factor: humanity must make a moral about-face'. The Church must take the lead in making this about-face (Mette). To work for peace it must promote and work for justice, for only to the degree that there will be liberty and justice for all will there truly be peace in our world (Jegen). Because the Church is the agent of life it must work for peace. Not a simple task, but certainly the indispensable one.

As a synthetic theological conclusion to this issue, there is an article (by Schillebeeckx) in which attention is given above all to the inner and positive relationship between the 'peace of Christ' and the historical, social and political peace that has to be built up by men and women on the basis of a more just political economy. In this article, the author contrasts the ideology of the politics of safety followed by modern States with the radical protest of the Gospel. It cannot, however, simply be allowed to rest at the level of a moral appeal. Political praxis on the part of Christians can in fact give a social and political content to Christian hope in terms of a policy of historical peace. It is from this vantage-point that the delicate question is finally asked as to whether the Gospel can call on us to take steps towards unilateral nuclear disarmament if all the other means fail and, in view of the immanent logic of the strategy of deterrence, even fail fundamentally.

VIRGIL ELIZONDO
NORBERT GREINACHER

Paul Peachey

Anthropological and Sociological Reflections on Human Aggression and Social Conflicts

INTRASPECIFIC VIOLENCE, sometimes described as 'man's inhumanity to man', is a baffling trait of *Homo sapiens*. The cruelty of human beings to human beings, is it innate or accidental? Much historical evidence can be interpreted as supporting the former conception, that such cruelty is indeed innate. War, genocide and mayhem appear far too widespread and recurrent to be regarded as merely accidental or aberrational. On the other hand, such phenomena are by no means universal. Intraspecific violence occurs neither always nor at all places. Moreover, a 'killer instinct' in man, as we shall see, is at odds with 'human nature' otherwise.

Paralleling, and perhaps mirroring, this paradoxical evidence is the ambivalence regarding war we find in human culture and consciousness. The horrors of war repel, yet they also fascinate. Despite the overlay of myth and pretence involved in military legend, military exploit appeals to something primitive and irrational within the human psyche. This 'something' is doubtless a powerful factor in the perpetuation of the war system in civilisation.

Attitudes and culture themes, however, are subject to shifting moods. If there are times when a psychosis of war may dominate the reality perception of a particular society, at other times, when the grim realities of war are more immediately at hand, a period of revulsion may set in. The early years of the nuclear era were such a time. During the 1950s when the hydrogen bomb was first tested and deployed, masses of people in many lands responded in consternation. 'Nuclear pacifism'—the view that military strategies and actions based on nuclear weapons must be rejected on moral grounds—became an option for many people who otherwise accepted the legitimacy of conventional armaments. Eventually a policy compromise emerged which seemed tacitly acceptable to political majorities: nuclear weapons came to be tolerated temporarily as a means of deterrence as the lesser evil on the assumption that in fact they will not be used in combat. This policy, it is readily evident, is inherently ambiguous and unstable. Weapons will have a deterrent effect, if at all, only if the possibility exists that they will be used. Nonetheless for about two decades, political majorities seemed to accept some version of the deterrence theory on the above grounds, a compromise further mollified by the willingness of governments to talk about arms control.

1

A combination of developments at the end of the 1970s and the beginning of the 1980s triggered a crisis of confidence in the balance of terror which had developed meanwhile. Prominent among these were hints emanating from official sources that actual strategic or combat use of the 'nukes' was being contemplated. Decision-makers spoke publicly of the possibility of 'fighting' and 'winning' a nuclear war. Such discussions, however, served only to alarm many political constituencies, and in a number of countries movements demanding an immediate 'freeze' in the further deployment of nuclear weapons suddenly became politically volatile. Political leaders were compelled to take the mounting public pressures into account. At this moment, however, it is not clear that this public clamour is sufficiently focused, or that it has the staying power necessary to effect basic changes in policy (the dismantling of the nuclear arsenal). Proponents of 'strong' nuclear policies expect this opposition, like earlier protests, once more to fade. Freeze advocates, on the other hand, looking for staying power, confront the question: How can the momentum of opposition to the nuclear weapons race which emerged in the early 1980s be maintained? Are we at long last at an historical turning point where the popular determination can effect a fundamental change in the way nations conduct their affairs?

Until the twentieth century, reflection on international relations was dominated by normative thought. Political theorists sought variously to describe ideal polities and/or interstate systems. The great religious traditions all contain visions of a world at peace which have had some modifying influences. All, however, have been compromised by the assimilation of spiritual vision to earthly empire. In fact, at least in Western history, religious and secular establishments have frequently been allied in the suppression of the pacifist impulse. Moreover, while the Judaeo-Christian tradition projects an exalted vision of a coming reign of peace, that vision seems overshadowed by that same tradition's pessimism as to possibilities 'within history'.

During the present century, in the study of international affairs, attention has shifted increasingly from the *normative* to the *empirical* disciplines. Human communities are treated as natural systems, subject, therefore, to 'laws' paralleling those governing other phenomena in nature. An empirical understanding of the relations of power, for example, is thought to improve our ability to cope far more than does the projection of ideal blueprints. Many researchers are sustained by the hope or belief that as the empirical foundations of the political theory are strengthened, the techniques of peacekeeping can be perfected. In effect, ignorance and under-development rather than built-in flaws are assumed to be at the root of international anarchy. But we face the question: to what extent, and in what ways, are such expectations justified? Do the biological, social and behavioural sciences hold the key to a warless world?

1. DETERMINISM AND SOCIOCULTURAL REALITIES

A wealth of specialised data on aspects of human conflict, aggression and violence has been generated by the various sciences. The usable yield however—usable in terms of collective action or public policy, remains disappointingly limited. As someone observed in another connection, this corpus of material consists of all limbs and no head. The difficulties are inherent, both in the scientific enterprise and in the nature of the problems of conflict. We shall sketch these difficulties briefly.

The sciences advance by increasing specialisation both among and within disciplines. The methods of investigation are reductionist. In a mechanistic universe, the 'cause' of war, for example, might be discovered in that fashion. Even in a dynamic and open universe such inquiries are useful. Something is to be learned, for example, from a comparative study of the events which precipitated the outbreak of hostilities in a given sample of wars. On the other hand, the 'causes' of any given war are far deeper and more complex that the precipitating event. Hypothetically one might argue that wars could be avoided if the precipitating event could be eliminated. But how is that to be done since the precipitating event takes on that quality only in or after the fact?

In reality wars are highly complex and multicausal phenomena. Necessarily complementing the specialised investigations proper to science, work of a synoptic sort, adapted to configurations of events and relations, causes and effects, of violence and conflict, is poorly developed. Despite the low probability that early success will be realised, persistence in the effort is mandatory.

Beyond this methodological problem lies a substantive one: to what extent is human action accessible to scientific investigation? Sociology in particular, and the social sciences generally, are recent arrivals in the hall of science. Prior to the modern scientific revolutions, as already intimated, normative and ideal states dominated political discourse. Descriptive, anthropomorphic and mythical perspectives commingled. In the wake of the modern industrial, political, and scientific revolutions, the world of human action came to be regarded as part of the determinate world of nature. Human social behaviour, it was found, displays regularities which are independent of the strivings of individuals. Giants among the founding fathers such as Karl Marx and Emile Durkheim, though differing profoundly in their approaches, concurred in their focus on the social patterns which are independent of actor intentions. Social systems and structures 'determine' acts and events, and these systems and structures consist of determinate relations among causes and effects.

The discovery of society as a reality *sui generis*, however, exacted a cost which has not yet been fully absolved. First, the more structural explanations of human events were developed, the more problematic personal agency became. Strictly speaking, for example, human groups consist of systems of roles rather than of persons. Actions can thus be described as functions of such systems rather than as spontaneous inventions of actors. On the other hand, the more complex a social system, the greater the number of variables comprising it, and the greater the range and importance of personal agency. Personal agency, however, rooted as it is in individual subjectivity, is in some measure idiosyncratic. Subjectivity, moreover, is for science a problematic datum. The conflation of the human with the natural in any case tends to exclude from social analysis those dimensions of the human phenomenon which are *sui generis vis-à-vis* other biological species.

If on the one hand, the human was identified with the natural in the rise of the social sciences, on another plane a distinction was drawn between the biological and the social spheres. For the possibility of creating a social science depended on the identification of a corresponding subject matter. Thus it was important to put as much distance as possible between biology, for example, and the social sciences. As already intimated, there are substantive reasons for separation as well. Culture and learned behaviour distinguish *Homo sapiens*. This need to demonstrate the independent (from biology) variability of sociocultural phenomena contributed importantly, thus, to the conceptions of human being and society which informed the social sciences. The distinguished anthropologist, Ashley Montagu, argued a generation ago, that 'man is man because he has no instincts, because everything he is and has become, he has learned, acquired, from his culture, from the man-made part of his environment, from other human beings . . .'. Social phenomena, though an aspect of the natural world, are thus not reducible to their biological substratum.

To separate thus extremely the biological and social planes of *Homo sapiens*, though analytically and methodologically appropriate, nonetheless exaggerates. Recent developments in sociobiology represent a perhaps inevitable reaction and corrective. Here it is important to note the cost at which the social sciences acquired their birthright—an overly-deterministic view of the social universe, and an exaggerated distance between social behaviour and its biological base.

2. WAR AND HUMAN NATURE

Violence in human affairs assumes many forms, and occurs on various levels, both individual and collective. Our attention here focuses on the latter, notably on war. War is a social phenomenon, and is something other than the aggregation of the violence felt or expressed by individuals. Researchers do not agree on the nature or the origin of war. Some see war as originating in a primitive or primordial context—something akin to the theological notion of a 'fall'; others link war rather directly to the rise of civilisation. In this view violence increases as civilisation advances. There is also the question as to how often war was invented, or whether it spread by diffusion from a single (central Asian) origin.

Conflict traditionally received considerable attention in social theory. Conflict theory is one of the contending general theories in sociological thought. With antecedents in Greek thought, and direct roots in the Hobbesian tradition (seventeenth century), conflict theory treats conflict as the constitutive process in social organisation. Taking the egoism of the human individual as the basic datum in social life, order, in so far as it exists, is the product of struggle. The patterns of dominance and hierarchy which emerge solve (to a degree) the problem of order in human aggregates. Conflict theory offers itself as a preferred alternative to consensus theories, of which structural-functionalism has been the best known in recent times.

Marxism is the most comprehensive and fully developed conflict theory. Much of the appeal of Marxism is due, no doubt, to the fact that it offers itself as an alternative to the acephalous state of social theory otherwise (see above). The Communist Manifesto (1848) describes all previous history as class conflict. Though Marx's basic economic formula is arguable, his emphasis on what are now called the 'structural' sources of conflict and/or violence is one of Marx's lasting contributions.

If a common denominator with reference to violence is to be sought among the many, sometimes conflicting sociological theories now prevailing, it will most likely be found in reference to the structural genesis of conflict. Inequities in the distribution of wealth and privilege in society are regarded widely among social scientists inevitably as sources of conflict. Moreover, since political regimes (reflecting existing social inequalities) appeal to violent sanctions to defend authority violence may also be used to challenge authority.

The distinction between the 'objective' and 'subjective' dimensions of conflict has also been underscored. Failure to recognise this distinction can result in confusion. 'Objective' dimensions refers to structural incompatibilities which must be dealt with if conflict is to be resolved constructively or peacefully. 'Subjective' dimensions refer the attitudes of the actors in the conflict which may or may not be congruent with the objective dimensions. Conflict behaviour, and even violence, may occur without objective grounds, depending on the subjective states of given actors. Similarly objective conflict need not issue in conflict behaviour or in violence, if the parties possess the resources needed to reach solutions otherwise.

In the social sciences during recent decades in more specific terms, three principal, and competing, explanations for violence and aggression in human societies have been advanced: frustration-aggression, social learning, and biological-instinctual. The first of these theories posited a linear relationship between the frustration of goal-directed activity and aggressive acts. When aggression occurs, there has been antecedent frustration. When frustration occurs, a discharge of aggression necessarily follows.

Critised as overly-deterministic, frustration-aggression theory was soon modified to take into account the joint operation of other determinants.

The second of these explanations, social learning, largely reflects the heyday of the separation of the social from the biological sciences. Rejecting the notions of instinct as the root of aggression, and emphasising the importance of culture in the shaping of human character, social learning theorists accounted for aggressive and violent behaviour in terms of social process. Social learning theory rejects both the notion of fixed inner dispositions, of whatever provenance, or of stimulus events with invariant force in accounting for behaviour. Violence is a social outcome.

The third of these arguments, the biological-instinctual, is the most controversial. Though the idea that *Homo sapiens* has a 'killer instinct' is not new, it received a new lease of life in recent years, thanks to the impact of studies in ethology and primatology. The response to popularised treatments of an aggressive instinct in the human species by writers such as Robert Ardrey and Desmond Morris suggests a widespread proclivity in many social circles for such ideas. While at the present stage of research, many questions are unanswered as to the interaction of biology and culture in human development, the grounds are strong for rejecting the biological-instinctual theory of human aggression and violence: (a) the lack of empirical evidence for such an instinct: and (b) the minimal role of instinct in human endowment otherwise. Neither of these counter-arguments, however, has been, or can be, fully 'proven'. With regard to the first, the scientific method requires the operationalisation of all the elements in an explanatory calculus, as well as the possible falsification of any explanatory proposition. Such tests have not yet been devised with reference to the possibility of instincts. Meanwhile such evidence as we have is largely circumstantial. Nonetheless the view tentatively advanced here is that intraspecific human violence is not instinct-driven; we must account for it otherwise.

A more important argument than lack of evidence stems from a phenomenological approach to human being, sometimes described as 'philosophical anthropology'. Without foreclosing the philosophical and theological questions regarding evolution, special creation, and the like, it has been widely argued that deprivation of instinct, comparatively speaking, and therefore both the need and the possibility of culture, is what distinguishes the human from the other species. There are complex biological corollaries: early birth and prolonged dependency; large brain; bipedalism and the opposite thumb; and the like. Human being in effect is anticipated in human biology. Alongside the genetic legacy in the case of the human species has been placed a cultural one, perhaps with analogous evolutionary mechanisms operating in both spheres.

Not only culture is made possible and necessary by the biologically unfinished nature of human nature but subjectivity agency, and symbolic communication as well. Biological needs and drives persist nonetheless, and culture, whatever its higher symbolic content, is perhaps to a major extent the outcome of the adaptive processes of human beings in the 'natural' environment. Human beings are both rooted in nature, and destined somehow to defy, to transcend, and to supplant nature.

3. THE PRECARIOUS COSMOS OF *HOMO SAPIENS*

These few theories are by no means exhaustive. What we must note here is the fact that results in the social sciences so far lead away from, rather than towards, the expectation that a single explanation for aggression and violence in human affairs can be sought. This does not mean that attempts to identify or to measure specific variables or correlates linked to violence are futile. Below we shall argue quite to the contrary.

What this does suggest, however, is the need for greater clarity with regard to the basic issues of theory and methodology. If we recognise that the causes of violence generally, or of war particularly, are complex and multiple, our task is to determine the configurations of circumstances under which violence does or does not occur.

'Destructiveness and cruelty are not instinctual drives' Erich Fromm wrote in his last major work, 'but passions rooted in the total existence of man'. Ordering of the environment, provided by the articulation of instinct and environmental resources in other species, is left for human beings themselves to achieve. Indeterminancy, and hence freedom and insecurity are the human destiny. Nothing can be more threatening to human beings than the destruction of their cosmos, the set of definitions and expectations which they themselves create to fill the void left by their instinct-deficient biology. It is these definitions that provide security, both against unpredictable action by others, and against unchannelled or undefined drives within themselves. As a Marxist philosopher once remarked, the human animal posits meaning, and when meaning is denied, existence becomes intolerable. If he is right, we may well have a clue to an understanding of a great deal of violence and warfare.

Political rule has conventionally been territorially defined. Gaining monopoly of political power functions within a specified territory is the first task of a State/ government. Establishment of a rival entity, laying claim to political monopoly within the existing jurisdiction, is one condition no State/government can countenance. Territory is thus a critical specificum of the State, not because of some blind 'territorial imperative', but because territory appears as the most effective tool in the establishment, the definition, and the management of the prevailing set of social conceptions and expectations which order the existence of given human aggregates. The territorial tie is not for that reason instinctual in nature. In federal States, different authorities in fact operate within the same territorial unit. The commingling of authorities within territories grows in an increasingly interdependent global society, and may contribute importantly to the coming post-national era. Reasons for exclusive claims, by political authorities, in other words, are not *instinctual* but *human*.

Territoriality, along with spatial variables generally, remains a critical variable in all social life. It is one of the properties of the material environment readily available as a material coordinate of social interaction. Physical contiguity is a primary category in all human cultures: contiguity of residence spontaneously defines distance, closeness, and basic obligations. Spatial categories have provided thus basic dimensions in the definition of human community. Both with regard to the State and the locality, however, it is not territoriality as such, but territoriality as a symbol of variables critical to collective survival which account for the irrational collective power of territorial symbols. What appears to be at stake is the integrity and the perpetuation of the collective understandings on which the existing collectivity (social system, society) rests.

Direct physical contacts between human organisms occur continuously, but even then, social definitions intervene. Basically, however, human interaction involves complex processes of reciprocal interpersonal perceptions. Other people threaten the constructed world which we inhabit, not when or because their entry as such directly threatens us (though that may be the case), but when or because such intrusion implies to those intruded upon the undermining of the existing reality. In this respect the otherwise rather careless UN dictum—'War begins in the minds of men'—makes the critical point. An act is an act of war when it is so perceived by one or both (or more) parties.

4. THE FALKLANDS/MALVINAS WAR: A CASE STUDY

Analytically we thus confront a fairly abstract model of analysis. Application to a concrete case study may therefore be an important aid to understanding. The recent war in and over the Falklands/Malvinas, considered against the backdrop of the nuclear threat, appears well-suited to that purpose. The eruption of the South Atlantic crisis against the backdrop of the nuclear weapons debate produced some interesting analytical possibilities. Much about that crisis was reminiscent of the classic imagery of diplomacy and war in early modern times. In fact those dimensions of the case were pronounced enough initially to eclipse the serious nature of the conflict in progress. The question of interest to us here is the following: How was it possible, in a relatively brief period of time, both in England and in Argentina, to mobilise, if not galvanise, these populations around military-backed policies and courses of action which tended to be viewed by others in more relaxed circumstances in tragicomical terms?

To the Argentinians one might readily concede the going geopolitical logic: the location of the Malvinas suggests possible identity of interest between Falklanders and Argentinians which was hardly as self-evident in the case of Britain. To the British one might concede—despite the geopolitical arguments in favour of Argentina, the Falklanders were tied nonetheless ethnically, historically and politically to Britain. A forcible displacement by an alien regime this was surely a violation of sovereignty as popularly conceived. But a war, from either side, on these grounds alone? What additional variable accounted for the ostensible outrage of each at the other? If foregoing analyses are valid, and we offer them only as a working hypothesis, the critical variable in this conflict was neither a biological or social determinism, in any direct or linear sense, but the respective threat which each society saw in the action of the other to its own core reality. The perceptions were by no means spontaneous. Historical, national, and military myths operated as powerful conditioning forces. But there was nothing 'blind' or 'inevitable' about the South Atlantic dénouement. Political leaders, themselves prisoners, to be sure, of the same mythology, made decisions and manipulated the symbols of collective self-definition in ways which set the two governments on a collision course. Not, it can be argued, that the débâcle was due to lack negotiating know-how. No, what was and remains problematic is to be sought, as Fromm suggests, in the human domain, in the ways we construct and misconstruct our interhuman reality.

5. SOME GENERALISATIONS

Here I shall summarise results scattered through the foregoing parts of this article, supplemented and expanded by excerpts from some empirical studies.

(a) Conflict, when defined as multiple and (at least partially) mutually exclusive ends or interests, is inherent in human existence. Hostility, aggression, violence, and the like, on the other hand, though conflictual in character, are conditional or *accidental* rather than *innate* human phenomena.

(b) The sources of 'man's inhumanity to man', of aggression, violence and war are best sought in the precarious position of *Homo sapiens* (partly determined, partly free) in the cosmos, rather than in biological or social determinism. This view, held by many but not by all social scientists, does not deny the existence of such determinisms, but asserts only that war, or any other form of violence, represents human action rather than necessary or determined behaviour. (Thus, while prediction of the early eradication of war could be irresponsible, it is equally misleading to accept war as a fatal necessity.)

(c) Given current studies in primatology, ethology and socio-biology, the force of the genetic legacy in human social behaviour is undergoing review. Again, though there are disagreements, and false starts, genuine new evidence bearing on the interface of the biological and the social can only be welcomed.

(d) War and other forms of collective violence, though arising on the foundations of biological needs, drives, and resources, represent socially learned and/or generated behaviour. The acquiescence of vast populations to war, and their psychological availability for military mobilisation demonstrates the nature and the power of the human social heritage. It demonstrates as well the need for the cultivation of the processes of individuation and the personal agency in contemporary societies. Mass psychologies and stampeding impulses must be challenged by autonomously critical individuals. When war is accepted as inevitable, and preparations and capabilities for war become institutionalised, the sociocultural momentum is all but irresistible. At this juncture the 'realists' gravely observe that 'the world is a dangerous place', that disarmament is folly. As a result, prophecy fulfills itself. Sooner or later, 'aggression' occurs, and 'realists' can always be shown to have been right!

(e) Where the theoretical basis for research is adequate, empirical investigations can contribute enormously to our understandings of both the aetiology of violence and the processes of peace. Vast bodies of data exist, for example, which link insecurity (of the persons or groups) to aggression—or violence-proneness; on relationships between violent sports and hostility levels in populations; on effects of violence in the mass media on behaviour particularly of youth, etc. . . .

(f) Meanwhile the applied discipline provides perhaps the most practicable and accessible resources in areas other than military. New institutions, based in part on newly-developing meditation techniques, are developing for the solution of domestic and community disputes. Historically the development of national (central) legal systems appears to have atrophied local informal conciliation processes. Given the general renewal of interest in local democracy, the time appears ripe for the revitalisation of personal and local conflict-resolution processes. Study and training programmes at several levels—lay, paraprofessional, and professional—have much to contribute.

(g) The continuation of diplomatic and defence establishments appears inevitable in any foreseeable future. On the other hand, the sense of inevitability inherent in that assumption paralyses our collective will, thus guaranteeing the very inevitability we claim to fear. The supreme tragedy of the era is our inability to assemble our many capabilities into idioms of collective action. Thus the energy generated in 'nuclear freeze' and other initiatives cannot be harnessed productively for sustained peacemaking action and the structural changes required. The questions persist: Why?

François Houtart

Armed Conflicts and Economic Aggression: North-South Relations as a Form and Factor of War

WORLD OPINION is rightly worried by wars and armed conflicts. Even more important is protest against the insane arms race, particularly the nuclear arms race,[1] and against the fundamental distortion of political analyses and judgments which is both its necessary condition and its inevitable result. Nevertheless there are other forms of aggression, no less costly in human lives but less spectacular: the economic exploitation which makes it impossible to solve the vital problems of the Third World is the clearest example of these. This article will review various aspects of what are today called North-South relations in order to offer an analysis of them and to show the close connection which exists between these relations and armed conflicts, while not excluding East-West relations.

1. NORTH-SOUTH RELATIONS

The language used encourages confusion. It might be asked what is the nature of the relations described in this way. At first sight they seem to be geographical, but this is a fairly accidental aspect of the phenomenon if we are interested in understanding the essence. It might also be thought that what is at issue is relations between States, one group situated in the northern hemisphere and the other in the southern. With one or two exceptions this description is correct, but the political dimension of the problem remains superficial, important though it is. The term in fact describes economic relations, relations of production and exchange, which form the basis for the articulation of political relations and which hold between geographically identifiable collectivities.

But which economic relations are in question? It is clear enough that they are economic ties created within a market economy, between industrialised and so-called under-developed societies. These therefore exclude economic transactions between socialist regimes, but do include the economic relations established between the industrialised capitalist countries and the socialist countries of the Third World. It should be remembered that of Third World exports in 1976 28·5 per cent went to the European Community, 20·6 per cent to the USA and 2·2 per cent to the USSR.

Having defined the area, let us tackle the subject itself by recalling some facts about the southern hemisphere. Though they have over 50 per cent of world population, the countries of the Third World are responsible for only 15 per cent of production,[2] and the structure of income and of consumption shows enormous inequalities. In India, for example, which is the ninth industrial nation, almost 350 million people live in a state of absolute poverty, and 40 per cent of these are children under the age of ten.[3] In Bangladesh 80 per cent of the ninety million inhabitants exist on or below the threshold of this state of poverty. The cereal deficit of the Third World has tripled in twenty years, accentuating its dependence, and food production in sub-Saharan Africa has fallen by 10 per cent in a decade, at the very same time as its agricultural exports to industrialised countries have risen. According to the International Labour Organisation,[4] in the developing countries as a whole 100 million children work in conditions often resembling those of nineteenth-century Europe.[5] In Bombay 25 per cent of children start work between the ages of six and nine, and 48 per cent between ten and twelve. Some final figures: the World Bank estimates that 800 million people in the Third World, 40 per cent of whom are children under ten, live in a state of absolute poverty,[6] and UNICEF states that an average of 40,000 children die every day in the Third World from disease, malnutrition or hunger,[7] all of which are causes theoretically avoidable today.

The few figures quoted are first indices which help us to grasp the scale of the phenomenon and to discover the vast number of its victims, but secondly they can serve as the starting-point of our reflection. The figures themselves, of course, tell us nothing about the causes. It might be thought that the problem is simply delay in development, a problem time will solve, or that the causes lie mainly in the traditional patterns of pre-capitalist economies or in the cultural features of Third World societies. Without denying the complexity of the problems of under-development, it is nevertheless reasonable to suppose that the unequal distribution of consumer goods is not simply a natural phenomenon, but a social one, and that what some economists have called the plunder of the Third World[8] must certainly have results for the standard of living of the local populations. Moreover, when Third World countries put a stop to the logic of capitalist relations, they manage quite quickly to solve the problems of illiteracy, education, health and even basic nourishment, for the sections of the population which lacked them. This has happened in countries such as China, Cuba, and Vietnam and more recently still in Cape Verde or Nicaragua. We must therefore take a step further to examine the mechanisms by which situations are produced and reproduced.

2. THE MECHANISMS OF DOMINATION

Three key elements form the basis of the economic relationship between the industrialised capitalist countries and the Third World; *(a)* the supply of raw materials and sources of energy, *(b)* the opening of markets and *(c)* a new international division of labour which today affects production. All three are part of the logic of the accumulation and thus the maximisation of profit.

An increasing proportion of the *raw materials and base products* used in the northern capitalist countries comes from the Third World, above all those involved in the processes of key industries (non-ferrous metals) and strategic manufactures. It is therefore essential, not only to ensure a supply, but also to obtain them on the best possible terms. The fixing of prices is distorted by the unequal relationship and by the divergent interests of the producers. Only in the case of oil, an energy source currently absolutely essential but concentrated in a few countries, was a price increase possible, and then not without the connivance of the big American companies seeking to increase their capital for expensive investments, among other things, in nuclear technology. It is well known that the prices paid for primary products and basic agricultural products (sugar, cotton, coffee), have constantly fallen when one looks at them over a long period and that the economic crises of capitalism have had as one of their main effects a collapse of prices and the depression of the economies of the producing countries and an increase in their indebtedness.

The *market* constituted by the developing countries is by no means negligible, since it constitutes over 20 per cent of the export market of the USA, Japan and of the European Community.[9] Capital goods and manufactured products have a tendency to rise in price, because of increases in certain factors of production and the constant needs for increased accumulation to meet the demands of new technologies. The financial flows resulting from the investments, loans and other transactions favour the capitalist economies of the centre, since the ratio often reaches 1:4 or even 1:5, even with government development aid.

Finally the third factor, *transfers of production*. The figures for the last twenty years show that the present tendency to transfer certain types of production to Third World countries goes no way towards meeting Third World demands for a transfer of technology or productive capacity. Contrary to what might be thought, it is the least developed countries which are the object of this transfer and not those who, in one way or another, have made a start in accumulation.[10] In other words, there is no tendency towards a new international division of labour such as is demanded by the Third World countries who are calling for a new international economic order. What is taking place is much simpler, a search for a low-wage area where obsolescent forms of production are developed in the best possible conditions (tax exemption, free trade zones, etc.), which does nothing to resolve the fundamental problems of underdevelopment: employment, creation of surplus value to improve living conditions, etc.

In order to create, consolidate and reproduce through time such a structure of economic relations, a certain number of political conditions are required. Within the countries, first of all, States must ensure the reproduction of economic relations, keep wages low, if necessary at the price of suppressing social (trade union) and political rights, and carry out infrastructural development as dictated by the economic interests of the metropolitan countries and not by the development of the majority of the population. But there is also the harmonisation of policies with the logic of world capitalist accumulation, which results in political and military pressure.

An example will make the argument clearer. In January 1982 a memorandum from the US State Department was presented to the president of the Republic of Honduras laying down the conditions for economic aid of $63 million and military aid of $15·3 million. The first condition concerned American firms in Honduras and called for the ending of the dispute between Texaco and the government; the oil company wanted to raise the prices of its products against the wishes of the Honduran authorities. Also included in the condition was a settlement of the dispute between the Honduran government and two American banks, the First National City Bank of Boston and the Citizens and Southern International Bank of New Orleans, whose assets had been blocked after the collapse of a local subsidiary. The second condition was the introduction of a dynamic programme designed to attract new foreign investment, a reduction in the civil service, a revision of price controls in order to eliminate the ceilings fixed for the prices of milk, bread, eggs and medicines. The third consisted in abolishing non-competitive enterprises and the superfluous activities of certain parastatals, the agrarian reform, forest development and industrial development agencies, measures tending to bring the activities of these bodies to a halt. The fourth condition was that supervision by the World Bank should be accepted to measure the effectiveness of foreign aid.[11]

In addition the International Monetary Fund was to grant a loan of $55 million, on condition that the economy should be stabilised by means of taxes. With the World Bank, it required that import substitution industries be discouraged and instead the country be opened to foreign investment (in fact American), which would find waiting for it cheap labour for industries exporting to the American market. During 1982 the military aid proposed was considerably increased, joint manoeuvres were organised between the US army and airforce and the Honduran forces, and work started on three US air bases. The object was no longer simply to arm a local government to contain internal social conflicts, as in El Salvador, but to incorporate Honduras into the strategy for destabilising the Sandinista regime in Nicaragua,[12] a regime which internally is trying to break with the logic of capitalist accumulation and externally is trying to escape from the situation of total economic dependence on the United States.[13]

An example such as this illustrates the mechanisms of domination. The picture is complemented by the systematic rejection by the countries of the North of the demands of the South, a rejection repeated at various international conferences in recent years, UNCTAD in Nairobi (1976) and Manila (1979), the FAO in 1974 and 1979, the conference on transfers of technology in Vienna in 1979 and the UN conferences on a New International Order in Lima in 1974 and New Delhi in 1979. The effects of the crisis fall brutally on the least privileged groups in the Third World. The crisis is the product of excess capitalist accumulation and cannot be solved in a capitalistic logic except by a reduction in the costs of production reflected both in pressure on earnings and the social provisions won by the working class in the industrialised countries and by a fall in the prices of the primary products or raw materials (copper, tin, coffee, sugar, cotton, cocoa, etc.) which are the main source of foreign currency for Third World countries. In addition the demands of the IMF in its lending policy towards these countries consist in extracting an increased quantity of surplus value from the bulk of the population by bringing about increases in the price of basic foods and the abandonment of welfare policies. This was the IMF's position in Sri Lanka, where the government agreed to take these measures, and in Tanzania, where it refused and was deprived of economic aid.[14]

The fall in export earnings is also the origin of the catastrophic indebtedness of certain countries. It is true, for example, of Central Africa, where in a few months the price of sugar, to give only one example, fell from twenty-six to six US cents a pound.[15] Another factor is a reduction in technical assistance (nearly $2 billion in 1981), mainly due to cuts in US aid, which fell by 26 per cent.[16] The great paradox is that at the very time when some spokesmen, including President Reagan, are advising the Third World to abandon all economic controls as a means of solving their development problems (at the Cancun Conference on the New International Economic Order), economic pressures and military intervention are becoming ever more frequent. The consequences for the less privileged classes in the Third World are catastrophic: hunger, disease, acute poverty, revolts, repression, conflict. It would be too simple to present North-South relations as relations between States, some rich and some poor. The analyses must be taken further.

Countries are not composed of socially homogeneous groups nor are States socially neutral entities. Social classes are realities which form part of the very logic of a capitalist economy and State policies reflect the interests of those who exercise power. This explains why many underdeveloped countries are in fact run by oligarchies or bourgeoisies whose interests coincide, at least to a great extent, with those of capital in the industrialised countries, except that they demand a larger share of the surplus. The effects of the crisis, for example, are not the same on all sectors of society, either in the North or in the South. In 1972, when an earthquake destroyed Managua, the capital of Nicaragua, international relief was organised, from both public and private sources, to help the victims and reconstruct the devastated areas. The bulk of this was pocketed by the Somoza clan, which dominated the State, and profited vastly from it at the expense of other groups. In Zaire the endemic crisis does nothing to prevent a new class forming on the basis of an accumulation made by possible by its control of the State. In ways such as this networks of converging interests are created which form a world increasingly marked by class struggle on an international scale. But while the classes of capital, despite their internal contradictions, possess instruments of real integration (trans-national enterprises, communications), the worker and peasant classes remain essentially segmented and vulnerable. The countries in which popular forces have begun to break the logic of the capitalist economy are subjected to pressures ranging from the economic (Cuba, Vietnam, Mozambique), through the use of food as a weapon (Nicaragua, Vietnam, Mozambique) to direct or indirect military intervention (Angola, Mozambique).

3. EAST-WEST RELATIONS

It is very clear that East-West relations, even if they have their own characteristics, atomic weapons, relations between super-powers, etc., cannot be excluded from the discussion with which we are here concerned. The bulk of armed conflicts since the Second World War have taken place in the Third World and have been associated with East-West tensions and sometimes even armed conflicts (Korea, Vietnam, Angola, El Salvador, Lebanon). In addition to their immediate causes, which have generally attracted most attention, these conflicts have revealed the underlying reality of world economic relations and what it costs to break the laws of capitalist accumulation. It is in this sense that North-South relations are indeed factors making for war. Whatever judgment one wishes to pass on the economic and political systems of the socialist countries and whatever the contradictions which characterise them or the conflicts which divide them, it must be admitted that they have constituted a serious obstacle to the reproduction of capitalist relations in the regions of the 'South' by providing support—political, economic and, in the case of aggression, military—to many liberation struggles and to the regimes which have resulted from them.

4. CONFLICTING LOGICS

So far we have tried to show the reality of North-South relations and their effects on the life and death of hundreds of millions of people in the world today. For this purpose we chose to emphasise what goes beyond the phenomena of aggression or power-seeking, beyond what has always existed in the history of humanity, in order to highlight the economic mechanisms which give rise to structures of exploitative relations. This led us to show that what is taking place is a class struggle in which capital today possesses considerable economic, political and ideological weapons, which it uses above all where it feels itself vulnerable, though without renouncing military means. Nevertheless we still have to ask what is the logic which governs such courses of action; if we do not, we may lapse into explanations of a purely psychological or even purely voluntarist type, which in this case are totally inadequate.

This logic is the logic of capital as a dynamic factor in production, the result of an accumulation which can never be self-contradictory and which draws its existence from the extortion of surplus value, on the one hand from local labour and on the other from the exploitation of the societies it dominates. That is what makes Michel Beaud say, 'Capitalism is neither a person nor an institution. It has no will; it makes no choices.

It is a logic at work through a mode of production, a blind, stubborn logic of accumulation.'[17] Ever since its formation the capitalist system has included the exploitation of pre-capitalist societies. In the regions which we today call the Third World, the process began by the mercantile plunder of Latin America, Africa and Asia, which made possible the acceleration of the process of primitive accumulation, which eventually was to give rise to industrial capitalism. From the beginning there was a transfer of both wealth and labour. We need only remember the slavery of the Africans who were taken to America. The colonial phase of the nineteenth century made the nation-States the principal agents of this double extraction, and to the 50 or 60 million Africans who died in the slaving adventure we must add the tens of millions of dead of the colonial wars, the local revolts and the famines due to the disruption of traditional rural economies.

Today the basic units of capitalism have become enormous and go beyond national limits, but the logic is still the same, to extract surplus. Of course the system carries within it its own contradictions, the reaction of the social agents in the exploited classes, and this is what we are witnessing today. It was this which enabled the European and United States working class to improve its purchasing power, but compensation was available for this during the post-war economic boom in the form of a levy, above all on the peasantries of the Third World.[18] The pauperisation and proletarianisation of these peasants is in turn the origin of the social movements of almost the whole of Asia and Central America. This process encounters a different logic, which becomes an alternative programme, that of organising a mode of production in which the logic of capital does not necessarily lead to the sacrifice of millions of lives in the service of an accumulation which allows capital to continue reproducing itself and overcoming its crises.

Translated by Francis McDonagh

Notes

1. In January 1982 Mr Weinberger, US Defence Secretary, announced an increase in arms expenditure from $182 billion in 1982 to $326 billion in 1987, or an increase in the size of the army of 53 per cent, in the number of aircraft carriers by 69 per cent, in airforce spending by 58 per cent and the production of 37,000 additional nuclear warheads (Casper Weinberger, 'Remarks Prepared for Delivery Before the Council of Foreign Relations', New York, 20 April 1982).

2. Michel Beaud *Histoire du Capitalisme, 1500-1980* (Paris 1981) p. 287.

3. John Blair 'Aucune réponse à Cancun pour les 800 millions de "pauvres absolus" de la planète' *Imprecor* 112 (9 November 1981) 24.

4. *ILO Report*, Geneva 1969.

5. *Le Monde*, 13-14 September 1981.

6. World Bank report quoted *Imprecor* 112 (9 November 1981) 24.

7. UNICEF report, Geneva 1979.

8. P. Jallay *Le Pillage du Tiers-Monde*.

9. *Time Magazine* 37 (13 September 1982).

10. J. Petras 'A new international division of labour?' *Merip Reports* 94 (February 1981) 28-29. Note that countries such as South Korea, Taiwan and Hong Kong are exceptions because of the strategic aims pursued there.

11. *Le Monde Diplomatique*, May 1982.

12. This policy consists principally of arming Somoza's former National Guard to encourage incursions into Nicaragua. It will be remembered that the CIA received more than $200 million to destabilise the Sandinista regime.

13. The food weapon was used against Nicaragua; US grain shipments were halted. The EEC and the USSR replaced the US as grain suppliers in 1981.

14. The Third World countries want the UN General Assembly to be the supreme authority in these matters, but the industrialised countries, which are in a minority, insist that the management of these programmes be entrusted to the World Bank or the International Monetary Fund, which they control.

15. Whereas the capitalist market prices for sugar have fallen, the prices paid by the USSR remain stable, since they are calculated on the basis of 100 products sold by the USSR to Cuba: if these rise, the price of sugar rises too.

16. *Time Magazine* 37 (13 November 1982).

17. M. Beaud, the work cited in note 2, p. 161.

18. M. Beaud, *ibid.*, p. 252.

John Linskens

A Pacifist Interpretation of Peace in the Sermon on the Mount?

'DO NOT resist who is evil' (Matt. 5:39) and 'Love your enemies' (Matt. 5:44; Luke 6:25). These are demands of the Law of the Kingdom which seem to call into question the 'normal' human behaviour in conflict situations.

The established bourgeois order in the West feels that a literal fulfilment of these radical commands would mean the destruction of the 'human' society, i.e., *their* society. Do they not need the power of punishment and retaliation to maintain and defend that society?

For the oppressed such demands could precisely contribute to maintaining and strengthening a society they would like to change.

If we want to face this problem seriously we have to realise that such commands came into being and developed in particular historical situations. These situations were not the source of these sayings, but they were the context in which they functioned and made sense for those who believed. Nothing can be said about the normative value of these visions of the reign of God without reference to their historical situations. Faith obedience towards the coming reign could not be practised in the abstract then, neither can that be done now.

The message of Christian love calls for opposition against evil, but this opposition can take different forms in different concrete situations.

It is, therefore, necessary to retrace the tradition of the gospel compositions in which these sayings occur. Can the situation in which they functioned be more closely established? The so-called sociological approach to New Testament research can certainly be of great help in this area.[1]

1. THE LITERARY ANALYSIS OF MATTHEW 5:38-48 AND LUKE 6:27-36

The reconstruction of the course of a tradition is usually conjectural to some extent. But an effort has to be made for a responsible exegesis with acceptable conclusions concerning the successive stages of a tradition. Matthew has two antitheses: 'It has been said . . ., but I say to to you' (Matt. 5:38-42 and Matt. 5:43-48). Luke has some of the material of Matthew's first antithesis within his one composition about love for one's enemy (Luke 6:29-30/Matt. 5:39b-42). Matthew's sequence is certainly more original.

16

Luke 6:29-30 initially was not connected with 6:27f. The verses 29-30 are addressed to one person, whereas the verses 27-28 and 32-34 are addressed to a group. Besides, Luke 6:32f. clearly refers back to 6:27-28, and not to 6:29f. It seems probable that Matthew and Luke reflect the same form of Q.

It is to be noted that in 6:35 Luke resumes the statement of 6:27: 'Love your enemies.' He did not want to give up the *immediate* connection between the principle of love for the enemy and the promise of divine sonship, found in his source. In Matthew 5:44-45 we have this immediate connection. Matthew in his sequence is again more original when he has: first the principle of love for the enemy (Matt. 5:44), second the promise of divine sonship (Matt. 5:45), and third, the sayings about not only loving those who love you (Matt. 5:46-47). Luke gives this third part about loving not only those who love us before he resumes the principle about love for one's enemy (Luke 6:32-34 in front of Luke 6:35). He had interrupted the connection between this principle and the promise of divine sonship. He continued to insert more material (Luke 6:32-34), facilitating the return to the second expression of the principle in Luke 6:35.[2]

Other differences in the texts can be dealt with later. For the time being it is enough to know that the Matthean *sequence* is more original. The question remains, however, whether Matthew created the antithetic formulas since they only occur in the gospel of Matthew. This form is related to the Mosaic typology of the gospel of Matthew. At any rate, the two last antitheses (Matt. 5:38-42 and 5:43-48), are nearly unanimously ascribed to Matthew. In Luke 6:27-36 the same logia do occur without the antithetic preface. We think, therefore, that the Q source did not know the antithetic formulas.

2. THE TRADITION HISTORY OF MATTHEW 5:38-48 AND LUKE 6:27-36

(a) Non-Resistance on the Level of Matthew's Redaction (Matt 5:38-42)[3]

Attention should be paid to what Matthew has over and above the Lucan parallel.

There is the remarkable statement in Matthew 5:41: 'Should anyone press you into service for one mile, go with him two miles.' As a rule the verb used here (*aggareuoo*) does refer to a service forced upon people by the State. It has this meaning in Mark 15:21. Besides, Matthew uses here a Latin loan-word for the distance: *million*—a mile. The Romans forced conquered nations to render such services. Matthew's gospel was written for Jewish-Christians in the Galilean-Syrian region after AD 70 where the Romans were dealing with a defeated nation to which Matthew's Christians belonged. Flavius Josephus recommends non-resistance to the Jews, when Romans do injustice to them (*B. J.* 2,350-352). The idea of non-resistance was, so to speak, in the air. Matthew gives it a deeper theological foundation. It becomes in this concrete situation a manifestation of the kingdom of God. This is particularly clear in the next antithesis on the love for the enemy, of which the principle of non-retaliation is also a manifestation. Besides, this logion of Matthew 5:41 (just as Matt. 5:36b-40) does not simply recommend passive non-retaliation, but some sort of active non-retaliation: do more than what is demanded, voluntarily. We are inevitably reminded of Romans 12:21: 'Be not overcome by evil: but overcome evil by good.' This is not just the common sense attitude of the little man who does not retaliate because he is powerless. It is the power of non-violence which involves insurrection and resistance. It is the non-violence of Martin Luther King who chose this way as the best in the given situation: the best way to love the enemy and to invite him to change.

Matthew introduces these verses about overcoming evil by good (Matt. 39b-41) with the following antithesis: 'You have heard that it was said, "An eye for an eye, and a tooth for a tooth." But I say to you, "Do not resist one who is evil"' (Matt. 5:38-39b).

The Old Testament texts Matthew refers to are about the so-called *ius talionis* (Exod. 21:23-25; Lev. 24:19ff.; Deut. 19:21). Matthew understands these texts as an incitement to violence. The New Testament antithesis is strong: '*Do not resist the evil one!*' Remarkably Matthew only expresses the last three antitheses with such *apodictic* commands after the formula: 'But I say to you.' They are directly formulated in the second person plural. Are they not addressed to a particular group? And this antithesis about non-retaliation is also to be placed in the same life situation as verse 41. It was the only possible response of an utterly defeated people. It can hardly be denied that Matthew's Christians, socially and politically speaking, were underdogs. In the light of the gospel, however, they understand themselves as superior, as standing above the never-ending circle of violence and counter-violence (Matt. 5:20). They are promised to be sons of the Father in heaven (Matt. 5:45). And they should be perfect as the Heavenly Father is perfect (Matt. 5:48).

This superiority is their active non-resistance (which is a form of sublime resistance) expressed in the following verses (Matt. 5:39b-42). Some of these logia do not directly reflect the Matthean life situation, since they derive from the tradition. But they clearly express the *active* 'pacifism' of which the specific Matthean logion (v. 41) indicates the *Sitz im Leben*.

(b) Love for the Enemy on the Level of Matthew's Redaction (5:43-48)

Quite obviously the last two antitheses in Matthew (5:38-42 and 5:43-48) are closely connected, just like Matt. 5:27-30 and 5:31-32. The principle of active 'pacifism' is a case of active love for the enemy. This is important, because in the sixth antithesis a deeper, specific Christian rationale for this attitude towards the enemy is given. It is undeniable that this sixth antithesis contrasts the Christian understanding of love of neighbour with the Jewish understanding. The same antithesis to Judaism appears in the texts about the great commandment (Mark 12:28-34 and par). *Jewish* antagonism against the enemy (outsider), quite understandable in the historical situation of inhuman oppression, should on principle be impossible for Christians. They have the promise of becoming children of the Father in heaven (Matt. 5:45) and are told to be perfect as the Heavenly Father is perfect (Matt. 5:48).

Let us now have a closer look at Matthew's last antithesis about love for the enemy. It was already noted that Matthew seems to have a particular group of people in mind and now Matthew specifies this love for the enemy: '*Pray for those who persecute you.*' The idea of 'praying for *persecutors*' seems to suggest that we are dealing here with people who persecuted the Christians *as* Christians.[4] Matthew certainly often thinks of rabbinical Judaism as hostile to Christianity rather than of the Romans. But it cannot be assumed that for the Romans it was so easy to clearly distinguish between Jew and Christian, even after the great war. The Christians in the Palestinian homeland wanted to maintain their status as *Jews*. Why would rabbinical Judaism have struggled so hard to make *others* aware of that distinction? And why would they have been on their guard against Christian 'infiltration', if Jewish Christians had not tried to be seen as a part of the Jewish world? It can hardly be denied that Jewish Christians, as true patriots, must have joined the Jews in the great war against the Romans. The even did so sixty years later in the revolt of Bar Kokeba. It is not so unthinkable, therefore, that the Romans treated them the same way as the other Jews in Palestine. Besides, the love for the enemy, of which this antithesis speaks, is not to be separated from the injunction against retaliation in the preceding antithesis. It seems to be rather arbitrary to deny the possibility that on the level of the redaction Matthew thought of Romans when he wrote about 'persecutors'.[5] Praying for persecutors is again not merely passive resistance. It implies an invitation to these enemies to change their attitude. It witnesses to a missionary attitude to win such an enemy for the community. It is an aggressive love.

'So that you may be sons of the Father in heaven, who makes his sun rise on the evil and the good, and sends rain on the just and the unjust' (Matt. 5:45).

Sonship of God depends on acting like God, *the Father*. In Judaism imitating God means acting in accordance with the Torah. Here it means acting according to Christ's authoritative statement on loving one's enemy, which is contrasted with the Torah as handed down in the synagogue. Every person can observe when the sun shines and when it rains that this Father is kind and loving even to his enemies. There seems to be a relation between loving one's enemy to become sons of the Father in heaven, and the beatitude in Matthew 6:9, where peace*makers* shall be called sons of God. It appears that the love for the enemy is not a passive attitude but an active struggle. Besides, in the following verse it clearly transpires that love for the enemy and prayer for the persecutors does not mean passivity. There is an active effort to overcome evil by good.

'For, if you love those who love you, what reward have you? Do not even the tax-collectors do the same? And if you salute only your brothers, what is so superior in what you are doing? Do not even the Gentiles do the same?' (Matt. 5:46-47).

These verses relate the command to love the enemy to the requirement of a superior justice (Matt. 5:20). The behaviour of the true disciple is superior to that of the tax-collector and the Gentile. It is surprising that here the tax-collector and the Gentile are all of a sudden treated as the outsiders. It sounds very Jewish, and can hardly be placed on the level of Jesus himself, the friend of the tax-collectors and outcasts. But does such a phrasing not become very meaningful in a situation where tax-collectors were seen as the friends of the pagan Romans who harassed the Christian Jews? These expressions certainly functioned very well on that level.

They think in terms of a *quid pro quo*. Loving one's enemy precisely means going beyond that reciprocity. An active response, not some passive attitude, is expected on the part of the Christian; only then, they are superior. It is the superiority of the seemingly defeated, oppressed.

It all fits in with the life-situation which we think to be the historical context of the redactional meaning of the text. *'You, therefore, be perfect as your Heavenly Father is perfect'* (Matt. 5:48). The formulation is certainly Matthean (see Matt. 19:21). The Heavenly Father is obviously seen as perfect because he is totally and unconditionally God-for-men. He cannot exclude enemies, he cannot be restricted by the law of reciprocity. That is to be the perfection of the disciples.

(c) Love for the Enemy on the Level of Luke's Redaction

It has already been pointed out above that Luke's sequence in 6:27-36 is less original than Matthew's. Some material which is found in the fifth antithesis in Matthew (Matt. 5:39b, 40, 42) has been integrated in the one Lucan composition on love for the enemy. This Lucan restructuring causes the resumption of the commandment of love for the enemy in Luke 6:35.

Luke's life-situation has nothing to do with the situation of a defeated, humiliated Jewish people. His redaction is related to popular Hellenistic ethics. Luke brings out that Christian morality can compete with the world and is, indeed, far superior to it. Such a comparison is certainly not foreign to the thought of the third evangelist.[6]

There is another striking characteristic of the Lucan composition. Here as much as elsewhere in his gospel he is very much interested in 'financial' affairs. Luke omits for the time being the issue of borrowing from his own verse about giving to the one who begs (Luke 6:30; see Matt. 5:42). But then he gives it particular emphasis further on, where he speaks no less than three times about lending (vv. 34, 35). And where he resumes the principle of love for the enemy, he no longer repeats any of the examples of the verses 27-28, but mentions only one example: '*Do good and lend expecting nothing in return*'[7] (Luke 6:35). At the same time he is more radical than Matt. 5:42. He says that the Christian should lend without expecting anything in return (Luke 6:34, 35). For Luke the tensions among people arise from socio-economical relationships. He also radicalises (or eventually adopts from tradition) sayings in the same socio-economical area. He says that they should not withhold the undergarment from one who *steals* the uppergarment. He also says that they should (always) give to *everyone* who begs from them (Luke 6:30a). And finally he demands that they should not ask back what is *stolen* from them (Luke 6:30b). We are here in a different world, a world in which financial interests can cause violent oppositions.

The different Lucan life-situation is obvious. He situates the principle of love for the enemy in a situation of 'homo homini lupus'. He answers with Jesus' radicalism: 'Always give who begs from you'. Do not ask back from the one who steals from you', and 'Lend expecting nothing in return'.

Are they practical solutions to hatred and animosities in a 'capitalistic' world? They are gospel principles for those who will be sons of the most high (Luke 6:35), and who are told to be merciful 'as the heavenly Father is merciful' (Luke 6:36). They are about as practical as dying on the cross for others. But they are decisively efficient in as far as in their aggressiveness they do not allow an enemy to be an enemy. They invite him to change and respond. Such radicalism had an eminently missionary value.

(d) Love for the Enemy on the Level of the Q Tradition

It has already been established that the Matthean sequence is the sequence of the Q tradition. As far as details are concerned, we can find traditional formulations in Matthew as well as in Luke.

For the following verses we discuss those differences that are important for the content.

Matthew 5:40; Luke 6:29b. Matthew talks about a court case. Luke, however, deals with a robbery. Matthew's version could be an interpretation in a Jewish-Christian context. The issue of Luke could go back to the Q tradition. It would fit very well, in the life-situation of the Q tradition.

Matthew 5:41 (missing in Luke) reflects Matthew's life-situation. But it could belong to Q because it also fits very well in the Q tradition, as we will see later.

Matthew 5:42; Luke 6:30. The additional *pass = all* is typically Lucan. The verb *airein = to steal* (instead of *daineisasthai = to borrow*) is a radicalisation. Luke 6:34 proves that the idea of 'lending and borrowing' is more original.

Luke 6:31, the so-called Golden Rule, was most probably already connected with Luke 6:30 in Q.

Matthew 5:43-44; Luke 6:27-28. The antithesis is Matthean. 'Those who hear' in Luke 6:27 is redactional (see Luke 6:17). For the rest, Luke 6:27-28 is most probably more original. Luke did not create these four examples of love for the enemy.

Matthew 5:45; Luke 6:35c. 'Sons of the Most High' is certainly Lucan. Besides, in 6:36 Luke has 'your father'.

The image of the 'sun' and the 'rain' is primary to the more abstract Lucan *acharistos = ungrateful*.

Matthew 5:47; Luke 6:33. The term of popular Greek ethics '*agathopoiein = to do good*' is Lucan. It enables Luke to synthesise the preceding verses (Luke 6:29-31).

Luke 6:34 is certainly Lucan.

Luke 6:35. Luke resumes the theme of love for the enemy (6:27), after the insertion of 6:29-34. The connection is very Lucan, and the verbs used, all derived from the preceding Lucan verses.

Matthew 5:48; Luke 6:36. 'Merciful' is certainly more original than 'perfect' in Matthew (see Matt. 19:21). *Oun = therefore* is also to be ascribed to Matthew.

So the Q tradition must have looked like this (Matthean numeration):

Matt. 5:39: To you I say: To him who strikes you on the (right) cheek, turn the other one also.

40: And if someone steals your cloak, let him have your coat as well.

41: If anyone forces you to go one mile, go with him two miles.

42: Give to the one who begs from you, and do not turn down who wants to borrow from you.

(Luke 6:31): And as you wish that men should do to you, do so to them.

44: To you I say: Love your enemies, do good to those who hate you, bless those who curse you, pray for those who abuse you.

45: And you will be sons of your Father. He makes his sun to rise on the evil and the good and He sends his rain on the just and the unjust.

46: For if you love those who love you, what reward have you? Do not even the tax-collectors do the same?

47: And if you salute only your brothers, what reward have you? Do not even the Gentiles do the same?

48: Be merciful, as your Father is merciful.

The Q tradition as an oral tradition only survived as long as it served the interests and lifestyle of the *tradentes*, those handing it on.[8] Now it seems to be very clear that there are a number of radical sayings in Q which simply make no sense as instructions to Christians who live a normal family life. Such Christians cannot live as the lillies of the fields or as the birds of the skies. They are not supposed to leave father, mother, wife, brothers, sisters, etc. They cannot give up even the most minimal means of security. They cannot completely rely on the hospitality of others. We are not surprised that the extreme demands of the Q tradition are entirely missing in Paul's paraenesis to his Christians.

Who then took these radical sayings of Q seriously and tried to practise them? These sayings reflect an ethos of people without a home, without a family, without the minimum material means, and relying on others for hospitality and sustenance.[9] They are the wandering prophets who moved from place to place, from town to town, to evangelise people in the Syro-Palestinian region. Only for such people it makes sense to accept that kind of total apostolic renunciation. Only they could hand down such radical sayings without becoming incredible. Besides, already for a man like Paul, as it appears in I Corinthians 9, such a lifestyle became impracticable. But Paul also knew very well that he made an exception to the rule for prophets.

Considering, therefore, that this type of prophecy was the rule and that their lifestyle is unquestionably reflected in the Q sayings of the gospels, it would be, to say the least, very illogical not to connect the form as well as the content of these sayings with these wandering prophets. At least there should be no question for the oral stage of the Q tradition.

Now we can identify the life-situation of these particular sayings from their very nature.

'To him who strikes you on the cheek, turn the other one also. And if someone steals your cloak, let him have your coat as well' (Luke 6:29). The text speaks of a hold-up. It quite probably reflects the Q situation, for Luke himself is concerned with quite different problems.

Matthew 5:41 talking about the requisition of services for the State (in the context of Matthew theologically redactional) might go back to the Q tradition. Usually such a requisition included the draught animal (see Epictetus IV, I, 79).

Now in Matthew 5:41 no such animal is involved. The person himself only is forced to go a mile. Does that not reflect the situation of a wandering prophet? Besides, for him who was always on the go, going a mile further than he was forced to go was not so extraordinary after all.

In Matthew 5:45 nature becomes an example for man. Quite often it is said that such sayings are Wisdom sayings. The question is what their concrete life-situation was in Early Christianity. Does such a simile not remind us of other New Testament sayings such as the one about the lilies of the field and the birds of the sky (Matt. 6:25-36)? In the Jesus tradition they become positive models. Jesus' followers can be free from worries. It is their privilege not to work, even their right. The message of the kingdom is more important. All this fits in perfectly with the situation of the homeless, 'penniless', non-working charismatic wandering prophets.

Another more constructive approach can substantiate this life-situation of the Q document with more certainty. A literary analysis of the beatitudes (Matt. 5:3-12 and Luke 6:20-23) shows that four of these beatitudes belonged to the Q source. The fourth deals with the early Christian prophets, harassed and persecuted for their Christian witness (Matt. 5:11-12; Luke 6:22-23). There are differences between the two versions. It would be difficult to establish exactly the most original version. Besides, in this case it does not matter that much.[10]

Matthew speaks of persecution in 5:44, whereas Luke mentions hatred in 6:27, both within the composition of love for the enemy. There is a connection here in *life*. Love for the enemy is to be seen in the context of persecution and hatred. That the *Christian prophets* are meant is obvious from the texts themselves. Then how would it be possible not to connect the persecuted, wandering, homeless prophets of Matt. 10:23, 10:41 and 23:34 with those who are called blessed in Matthew 5:10-12 who are persecuted, reviled and falsely accused? Besides, the blessed of Matthew 5:10-12 are compared with the prophets before them.

Now this macarism derives from the Q tradition. Even if it were true that Matthew and Luke reduce the role of these wandering prophets, there can be no doubt about their role in the world of the Q tradition.

We conclude, therefore, that we have to read the Q tradition which lies at the basis of Matthew 5:39-48; Luke 6:27-36 in the light of this concrete situation.

The principle of love for the enemy and of an aggressive type of non-violence on the level of the Q tradition is to be seen in the context of the wandering prophets who were often chased from place to place.[11]

(e) The Historical Origin of the Principle of Love for the Enemy

Establishing the function of this principle on the level of the apostolic tradition does not mean determining the historical origin of the principle on the level of the historical Jesus. These two things should be clearly separated.

The question to be asked on the level of the historical Jesus is whether it is possible to distil an older tradition from the form of these sayings in the Q tradition. Most scholars deem this to be a rather hopeless undertaking.

The reconstructed Q tradition of the logia on non-violence (see above, (d)) is not a perfectly coherent set of sayings. There is a divergence in content.

It is a warranted guess that only Matthew 5:39-40 should be assigned to the oldest tradition.

When we consider the logia on love of enemy, on the Q level, Matt. 5:46f. par is most probably to be eliminated for more original tradition. Through form and content these two verses interrupt the close connection between Matt. 5:45 and Matt. 5:48. Moreover, v. 46f. can hardly be an authentic Jesus saying. In his preaching and his praxis he did not refer to tax-collectors and Gentiles in such a way.

It is possible that the oldest tradition had only one demand, the fundamental demand: love your enemy.

The earliest tradition must, therefore, have looked like this: '*To you I say: To him who strikes you on the cheek, turn the other one also. And if somebody steals your cloak let him have your coat as well. To you I say: Love your enemies (do good to those who hate you, bless those who curse you, pray for those who abuse you) and you will become sons of your father. He makes his sun rise on the evil and the good and he sends his rain on the just and unjust. Be therefore merciful as your father is merciful.*'

There is no reason for not ascribing the substance of these sayings to the historical Jesus.

This is all the more the case because there is continuity between the life-situation of the Q tradition and the life-situation of the historical Jesus. He, too, led a wandering homeless existence and he called people away from their home and trade to follow him in that prophetic wandering. They shared his mission to the poor and unrooted people to preach and demonstrate the kingdom to them first of all. His preaching of the kingdom apparently implied the proclamation of non-violence and love for the enemy. He asked his closest followers to practise this prophetic role in an exemplary way.

We can say, therefore, that Jesus' appeal for an aggressive non-resistance found somewhere a fertile soil: it was also tried by certain Jewish groups. But Jesus at the same time showed the courage of open critique. He acted provocatively and was dangerous for the 'establishment', Jewish as well as Roman. But at the same time he demonstrated and accepted a vulnerability, which was based on his special proclamation of the coming rule of God. It is this love and this acceptance of violence against himself that Jesus ultimately demonstrated on the cross. For believers the cross is the ultimate revelation of a non-violent active love even for the executioners.

3. THE FEASIBILITY OF JESUS' RADICAL DEMANDS IN MATT. 5:39-48 AND LUKE 6:27-36

On the question of feasibility of Jesus' radical demands Christians have been divided over the ages. A number of options can be distinguished. The so-called 'interim ethic' takes the heroic, literal fulfilment of Jesus' commands seriously for that short interim period without regard for the societal effects, for the simple reason that society is not going to last very long.

The so-called *Gesinnungsethik* takes the realistic, historical possibilities seriously and tends to reduce fulfilment of the commands to the development of a loving disposition. They seem to leave the world to its own 'normal' course.

The classical Catholic view takes sober account of human ability and the effect on society, if all Christians literally followed these commands, and it construes the literal fulfilment of them as a special task for a few.

Luther attempts to preserve both society and the strict fulfilment of the command by restricting literal fulfilment to those instances where only 'my' concern is at stake.

Certain visionaries today see the commands as standards for all relationships: personal, social and national. Literal fulfilment would transform all spheres of human life.[12]

The problem is nearly always looked at from a typical bourgeois standpoint. They are out to preserve *their* human society.

The victims of Western society, the oppressed, did not write biblical dissertations. The recommendations given to them from 'up there' cannot but look suspicious and self-serving. We can imagine them asking the question why theologians were so eager to create a theory of a just war, whereas not too many were eager to discuss the possibility of a just revolution.

What cannot be questioned on the basis of our analysis of the gospel-sayings on non-violence and love for the enemy, no matter how much disagreement there could be about the historical situations, is that these sayings functioned in concrete, historical contexts and the people who preached and heard them looked at the world from the standpoint of the oppressed and the marginalised.

This does not mean that they merely reflect the survival tactics of the underdog who would have no other choice. If that were the case they would be the same as the ethics for slaves recommended by pagan philosophers. In that case, Christian ethics would seem to be reduced to sheer situation ethics.

On the other hand, we are certainly not dealing either with absolute, abstract laws. Everybody agrees that would be a disastrous misinterpretation of the whole Sermon on the Mount and of all gospel ethics. St Thomas Aquinas, quoting St Augustine, had something to say here that everyone should take to heart: '. . . etiam litera evanglii occideret, nisi adesset interius gratia fidei sanans' (*Summa Theol.* 1a, 2ae, Q 106, a 2). The *gratia fidei sanans* is for St Thomas undoubtedly the Holy Spirit. What really matters is the Law of the Spirit of Life, the law of Christian love (Romans 8:3).

The law of Love is the basis of all concrete moral decisions. It transcends concrete historical circumstances, but is at the same time lived in concrete historical circumstances. It is the manifestation of the Life of the Risen Christ in his followers. In fact we can observe in the New Testament that this principle is the infra-structure of all ethical paraenesis.

It is precisely this new Christian foundation that makes the moral decision of non-violence and non-resistance in the New Testament more than a passive attitude. We are dealing with active 'aggressive' actions going beyond mere passivity. The 'adversary' is disarmed because he is loved in spite of everything. Martin Luther King and so many Christian prophets in Latin America give a striking witness of such non-violent, aggressive Christian love. And that is the foundational principle that cannot be relativised in any circumstances, or faith in the coming reign of the *father* in heaven would be given up. Hatred against the appalling violence of the establishment could never become the principle of a reform of the society. The exploited is asked to love those who he wants to change. That does not mean, however, that the concrete commands of the Sermon on the Mount should be unthinkingly transferred from one historical situation to another. They cannot be seen as absolute prescriptions. They are illustrations of what love of the enemy may and often should look like in the life of a disciple. That these illustrations are not always the way love of the enemy acts is clear from Jesus' own behaviour in the gospels.

We believe, therefore, that the demands of non-violence and non-resistance in Matthew 5:38-48 and Luke 6:27-36 do not prevent us now in 1983 from asking the question whether the principle of Christian love cannot lead to the decision of a justified rebellion of the exploited against structures which are created to perpetuate oppression and exploitation, provided that it is never inspired by hatred or revenge.

In some places the exploited and tortured masses stood up and changed the evil structures. Naturally, the paradise was thereby not regained. But the expected bloody revenge of the people against their former exploiters did not take place. The principle of retaliation of 'an eye for an eye and a tooth for a tooth' was never applied by the people. We hope that certain Machiavellian manipulations do not tempt the people into establishing some sort of dictatorship of 'the proletariat', which, as history proves, could be more repressive and harsher than some rightist dictatorships.

Notes

1. We recognise our indebtedness to the following scholars: G. Thiessen *Sociology of Early Palestinian Christianity* (Philadelphia 1978); *id. Studien zur Soziologie des Urchristentums*, WUNT 19 (Tübingen 1979); M. Hengel *Was Jesus a revolutionist?* (Philadelphia 1971); L. Schrotthof and W. Stegeman *Jesus von Nazareth, Hoffnung der Armen* (Stuttgart 1978); *id.* 'Non-Violence and the Love for One's Enemies' in *Essays on the 'Love' Commandment* (Philadelphia 1978) pp. 9-39; John Piper 'Love your enemies' in *Jesus' Love Command in the Synoptic Gospels and the Early Christian Paraenesis* (Cambridge 1979); P. Hoffmann *Studien zur Theologie der Logienquelle* (Münster 1976); P. Hoffman and V. Eid *Jesus von Nazareth und eine Christliche Moral* (Freiburg 1976).

2. See Helmut Merkein *Die Gottesherschaft als Handlungsprinzip. Untersuchung zur Ethik Jesu* (Stuttgart 1978) pp. 222-225.

3. For our view on Matthew's redaction see: G. Theissen 'Gewaltsverzicht und Feindesliebe (Matt. 5:38-48; Luke 6:27-38) in deren sozialgeschichtlichen Hintergrund' in *Studien zur Soziologie des Urchristentums* (Tübingen 1979) pp. 176-180.

4. John Piper, in the article cited in note 1, at p. 99.

5. Doubtlessly, Matthew also thinks of non-Jewish courts in 10:17-18.

6. See W. C. van Unnik 'Die Feindesliebe in *Lukas' Novum Testamentum* (1956) 184-300.

7. See G. Theissen, in the article cited in note 3, at pp. 180-183.

8. See G. Theissen 'Wanderradikalismus. Literatursoziologische Aspekte von Worten Jesus im Urchristentum' in *Studien zur Soziologie des Urchristentums* (Tübingen 1979) pp. 81-83.

9. G. Theissen, in the article cited in note 3, at pp. 183-191.

10. Jean Zunsteim *La Condition du croyant dans l'evangile de Matthieu* (Göttingen 1977) pp. 164-167.

11. For this view on the life-situation of the Q tradition: see G. Theissen, in the article cited in note 3, at pp. 164-167.

12. For the various interpretations of the feasibility of Jesus' radical demands, see John Piper, in the article cited in note 1, at pp. 96-97.

c

Gordon Zahn

Total War and 'Absolute' Pacifism

FOR FIFTEEN hundred years and more the major Christian communions have found it difficult, often impossible, to come to terms with what many see as inescapable pacifist implications of the faith they profess. Today the dilemma has been made more acute by developments in military technology as well as the emergence of nation/States which, at best, are religiously neutral but in situations of international strain or conflict inclined to resent any 'intrusion' of moral considerations into questions of policy. It was an American Secretary of State, not the representative of the officially atheist Soviet Union, who declared his viewpoint on negotiating crises as follows: 'The criteria should be hard-headed in the extreme. Decisions are not helped by considering them in terms of sharing, brotherly love, the Golden Rule, or inducting our citizens into the Kingdom of Heaven.'

The disparity between such pragmatism and the attitudes and practices of 'primitive' Christianity in the centuries closest to its founder and his earliest disciples is immediately obvious. The authentic Christian commitment then was to non-violence and to pacifism in an absolute sense. The English historian, Stanley Windass, has argued convincingly that the sense of being bound by the Gospel teachings of non-resistance to the evil-doer, coupled with self-sacrificial love, even for the enemy, was not the product of an 'aberrant stream of thought' but, instead, the *only* stream of thought. What some have advanced as evidence to the contrary—occasional and obscure references on Roman burial inscriptions, for instance—reflect individual behaviour, not community practice. As such they prove nothing beyond what anyone familiar with the weaknesses of human nature might take for granted: then, as since, Christians have not always practised what their Church preached.

The conversion of the Empire under Constantine brought a profound change, one which, as the preliminary draft of the American bishops' forthcoming pastoral on war and peace proposes, made it 'necessary' to consider under what conditions a believer might serve in the military. Though one might challenge the *necessity* of such a change in emphasis and direction, that it did take place cannot be denied. The appropriateness of St Maximilian Martyr's witness ('I cannot serve as a soldier; I cannot do evil. I am a Christian') was unlikely to be questioned by a persecuted minority which repeatedly witnessed 'brothers and sisters in the Spirit' carried away, tortured and even torn apart by ravenous beasts for the entertainment of a howling mob. In time it would seem less appropriate when such refusal was directed against an Empire which was now protector and promoter of Christianity. Still, it would be wrong to reduce the history of the 'Age of

Martyrs' to a simple and circumstantial expression of political dissent. The unwillingness of Maximilian and others to violate their consciences found deeper well-springs in the teachings and examples of Christ himself.

As those earliest Christians saw it, the rejection of all violence had its source in Scriptural instructions and incidents—in the Sermon on the Mount with its beatitudes; in the scolding of Peter for his impulsive resort to the sword; above all, in the passion and crucifixion and the call to take up the cross and follow him. These defined a new order of obligation. The old 'eye-for-an-eye' morality was overturned and replaced by readiness to forgive (seventy times seven times, if need be!). The Christian pacifism of succeeding generations unto our own continues in much the same vein, finding renewed confirmation in the models provided by Maximilian, Martin of Tours, and the multitude of martyrs and saints, known and unknown, who have given witness to its truth with their lives.

It is vital that we do not forget this history despite the theories and practices which have come to dominate the mainstream Christian churches in the post-Constantinian era. That original 'stream of thought' still flows and has found expression in the words and witness of inspired individuals and perfection-seeking communities down the centuries. Sometimes these have been rejected as 'heretic' and hunted down by the combined forces of Church and State. Since the Reformation they may have gained recognition (though not always toleration) as what we now call the 'historic peace churches'. Roman Catholicism, for its part, has found it convenient to make place, in its roster of honoured saints, for believers who lived lives marked by complete commitment and literal behavioural application of the Scriptural injunctions and counsels. On occasion, too, the continuity of Christian pacifism was preserved in the emergence of religious orders, the Franciscans being perhaps the most obvious example of this.

There is no denying, however, that such lingering adherence to pacifist tradition was overwhelmed by the acceptance and development of the concept of justifiable war introduced by St Augustine and given more precise and sophisticated elaboration by St Thomas and later Scholastics. The barbarians at the gates threatening the now converted Empire presented devout Christians with their first really crucial crisis of conscience. The simple and direct choice between mundane and eternal values was transformed into a choice between conflicting moral obligations, *both* of which were now invested with divine sanction. If too much has been made of the imperial oath as explanation of previous patterns of refusal, that concern was now negated by the declared obligation to obey legitimate authority in the person of a consecrated Christian ruler. Spiritual functionaries (priests, bishops and other 'holy people') were still expected, and later canonically obliged, to remain aloof from the bloodshed and violence of war, but the ordinary Christian who could not claim such special status or calling would be subject to ridicule, ostracism, and worse if unwilling to perform the duties laid upon him.

The 'just war' teachings were originally permissive and merely opened the way for the loyal Christian subject to serve in the military while still fulfilling his obligations as believer. It was an *exception* to the normal perspective on war which still implied the pacifism of the early Church. Unfortunately, but predictably, in practice if not in theory this restrictive character of the 'just war' formulation was generally ignored. In time, in fact, it was cancelled out by the principle which held that, in case of doubt, the presumption of justice was to be made in favour of legitimate authority. In effect this would all but exclude the possibility of what the sociologist would describe as religiously motivated deviance in time of war.

Theologians and moral philosophers in their insistence upon the immutability of natural and divine Law do not always welcome the intervention of the social scientist in areas over which they claim exclusive domain. Recent advances in scholarship, however, have made it clear that a deepened understanding of the situational, motivational, and behavioural dimensions of human behaviour have much to offer.

Certainly this is true with reference to the morality of war. Where the historian's work is essential to an awareness of the absurdities of the crusades as shocking evidence of how far reversal of Christian values had gone in the past, the political analysis of the rise and nature of the nation/State can demonstrate how close we are coming to making that reversal complete in our time. After all, the crusades, whatever else they may have been, were at least an expression of grotesquely distorted religious commitment. Contemporary wars on the other hand, though attempts may be made to give an idealistic gloss to their objectives and even assert divine approval and support, find their immediate justification in the defence (or acquisition) of territory and resources and the infinitely expandable demands of 'national security'.

Since the notion of a 'just' war logically implies the existence of an 'unjust' war, it introduced the option of a limited or 'selective' pacifism. If a war, to be justified, must meet certain carefully defined conditions, it should follow that any given war which does not must be denied the support and participation of the Christian. The scandal of witnessing the Mystical Body of Christ repeatedly torn apart as Christians fought on virtually every side of every war to come along suggests that logic did not always, or often, rule. To be even a theoretical option such 'selective' pacifism would be limited to those few who possessed the intellectual and theological sophistication required. And even so gifted a minority would find themselves hamstrung by that further 'principle' which granted the presumption of justice to the war-making authorities in case of doubt.

Of course, those few who refused to go along were not obliged to make their refusal public. The failure to volunteer the expected measure of support for the cause might evoke criticism or even condemnation as a sign of selfishness, cowardice, or worse. Nevertheless, it was possible for the 'selective' pacifist—should he or she so choose—to keep it a personal, and private, matter.

The advent of universal conscription, one of the crucial distinguishing characteristics of modern war, destroyed this possibility, at least for those made subject to military service. With conscription came a de-personalisation of loyalty. Now it was no longer a sense of the volunteer warriors' attachment to the leader and his cause, or, if that were present, it was not essential. Devotion to a charismatic leader (Napoleon, Hitler, etc.) might enhance commitment to the abstraction of 'the Fatherland' and its symbols, but it was that abstraction that held prior claim and had the power to enforce its demands upon the individual citizen.

Already between the first two world wars, a gathering of European theologians condemned Nationalism as 'the characteristic heresy' of our day, a judgment that has been validated and confirmed many times over since. A distinguished naval officer's sentiments expressed in a famous toast ('Our country, may she always be in the right; but our country, right or wrong') may be forgiven as an innocent display of theological ignorance or insensitivity, but to have those sentiments publicly endorsed by America's most prominent ecclesiastic in the context of the infamous war in Vietnam was a scandal of the highest order. No less shocking, and probably far more costly in its consequences, was the virtually unanimous record of active support for Hitler's wars on the part of German Christians and their spiritual leaders.

Few more glaring examples of the 'heresy' of nationalism can be found than the wartime pastorals of Germany's *Feldbischof* Rarkowski. On the occasion of his 70th birthday, for example, he reminisced upon the rebirth of the military forces under Hitler as 'a change for the better' and proceeded to praise the new era and its new young army 'which under its *Führer* and Supreme Commander has, since 1939, performed immortal deeds and reached the heights of accomplishment in offence and defence on all the battlefields of the present war.'[1]

Spellman, like Rarkowski, was designated bishop to the Armed Forces; but it would be a serious mistake to write such nationalistic excesses off as simply an occupational hazard. Though more restrained in expression, perhaps, similar sentiments were voiced by other bishops as well, not excluding some of the more heroic opponents of the Nazi regime. It is something of a cliché that political differences must stop 'at the water's edge' or where other national boundaries set the patriotic limit. It is a betrayal of Christian universality if the same should prove true of the application of moral principles in time of war.

The second defining characteristic of modern war—linked to conscription as both cause and effect—is that it has become total in nature and scope. The contesting combatants are now entire populations. Uniformed warriors have become but one resource among many to be exploited or attacked, and increasingly this resource has diminished in importance. In theory and in practice the concept of a legitimate target of hostile action has been expanded to include all persons or activities capable of making a potential contribution, no matter how indirect, to the maintenance of the wartime economy or national morale.

In 'total' war there are no non-combatants. The worker in the munitions factory; the farmer in his fields; the teacher in the classroom teaching the virtues of loyal citizenship; the housewife saving fats and cans; even the grade schoolchildren contributing pennies towards the purchase of a bomb—all are targets for destruction by weapons specifically designed to destroy them all. Is the day-care centre which frees mothers for work in the armaments factory not as legitimate a target as the factory itself? In the logic of total war, the answer is obvious. Ironically enough, even the pacifist is locked into the logic of total war: by refusing to pay taxes because they make him guilty of participating in the destruction and killing he deplores, does he not pass that same judgment upon his counterpart on the other side who fails to make the same refusal?

The reality of total war, in short, has reduced the 'just war' teaching and tradition to a pious fiction. Some, of course, might insist it never was anything more, but now at least the truth is there for all to see and acknowledge. Even 'limited' wars—witness Vietnam and Lebanon—have become 'total' in conceptualisation and execution.

For many Christians history has come full circle. Faced with the reality of total war, its strategies, and its weapons, the only appropriate response for those who would be followers of Christ becomes, once again, the absolute pacifism of the primitive Church. A world seemingly dedicated to its own annihilation offers no viable alternative to a rediscovered and renewed commitment to the non-violence preached by its founder. A worldly prudence which seeks security in the power and the readiness to inflict total destruction upon any potential enemy regardless of the risk to creation's future must finally yield to the Scriptural assurance that his power is perfected in human infirmity and the promise that the gates of hell will not prevail.

Between the two world wars Roman Catholic pacifists (a contradiction in terms some of their fellow communicants insisted) still put their case in the context of traditional post-Constantinian theology, rejecting war because it could no longer fit the conditions of the 'just war'. Often enough their arguments included an explicit disclaimer of absolute pacifism. Hiroshima shifted the balance. Some still use the 'just war' formulation, but the widespread tendency is to dismiss the concept as a redundancy, a regrettable compromise of the purity of Christian witness that is only now being recognised and corrected.

Contemporary pacifists are usually not inclined to engage in elaborate theological disputation. They are content with the unambiguous conviction that war in its nature is (and probably has always been) irreconcilable with the spirit of Christianity, a position they believe confirmed in Scripture and given literal application in the witness of the early Christians. What their interpretation may lack in intellectual sophistication is more than balanced by a deepened spirituality and sense of emotional commitment. Total war, in short, has brought a re-birth of absolute pacifism.

'Lord, it is true. We are not on the right path.' Pope Paul's lament in his 1970 World Day of Peace message finds its echo in the conviction held by Christians of the pacifist persuasion that the turning away from that 'right path' came with the acceptance of the concept of justifiable war. The rediscovery of that path, they will insist, requires a new theology of peace and non-violence and the readiness to accept sacrifice and suffering, even persecution, as the price for renouncing war and its atrocities.

Such a return to the Church's beginnings with the possibility of a second 'Age of Martyrs' raises the question as to whether modern Christians are prepared to meet such a challenge. The story of Franz Jaegerstaetter,[2] a simple Austrian peasant, gives reason to hope we can. In 1945 this heroic man, married and the father of three small children, was beheaded in Berlin for his refusal to serve in the Armed Forces of a regime he considered evil. Everyone—family, friends, neighbours, priests, even his bishop—counselled him to 'do his duty' as ordered, but nothing could shake his conviction that his first duty was to God and his Church regardless of the cost.

There is no way of knowing how many others may have died like Jaegerstaetter and for the same reasons only to perish without record. Maximilian, too, was but one among many martyrs most of whom are honoured only in the anonymity of the Feast of All Saints. The point is that many more might have taken that stand had they been called to it by their spiritual leaders, and the course of history could have been changed. As it was, this simple man had to take his stand alone aided only by his faith, by his conscious identification with the saints and martyrs he had taken as models, and by his firm conviction that for being true to his conscience he would merit at eternal reward in heaven.

There is one thing we do know, however. This peasant and any others who took that stand were more attuned to the true meaning of the Christian faith and promise than were the bishops who told the faithful to fight for Folk and Fatherland as a Christian duty. Whatever else the war and its horrors may have accomplished, it exposed the utter irrelevance of the just war tradition to the reality of modern war. The extreme in futility was reached in the opinion of one learned theologian that any judgment as to whether the war was just or unjust had to await its end when all the facts were in. In the meantime there was nothing to do but follow orders.

The Christian faced with the prospect of an even more horrible war, perhaps the ultimate war, cannot be satisfied with a theology which failed to recognise the injustice of Hitler's wars. They demand a better and truer answer, and for a growing number that answer is the complete renunciation of all war. In this they find encouragement in the words of the present Holy Father: 'The horror of warfare—whether nuclear or not—makes it totally unacceptable as a means of settling differences between nations.'[3]

Notes

1. G. C. Zahn *German Catholics and Hitler's Wars* (New York 1962) p. 151.

2. G. C. Zahn *In Solitary Witness: The Life and Death of Franz Jaegerstaetter* (New York 1964) *passim*.

3. Boston *Pilot* (16 July 1982); report of a talk by John Paul II in Rome on 12 July 1982.

Heinrich Missalla

'Für Volk und Vaterland': The Catholic Church and the German War Effort

1. THE 1933 CONCORDAT AND THE SENSE OF NATIONAL DUTY

IN ARTICLE 21 of the 1933 Concordat which the Holy See signed with the Third Reich the Catholic Church obliged itself to place special emphasis on education in national, civil and social duties in the spirit of the law of Christian faith and morals. A commentary on this obligation is provided by the *Manual of Contemporary Religious Questions* issued by Archbishop Conrad Gröber of Freiburg-im-Breisgau in 1937 'with the commendation of the entire German episcopate': a second edition appeared in 1940. In this we read: 'Our age is rightly concerned to overcome the bloodless, rootless intellectual approach of liberalism and Marxism, an approach that has broken free of all ties (see the entry on 'Enlightenment'). . . . Hence Catholic education will emphatically support every effort aimed at producing a sound, strong, capable, efficient person. It takes a positive view of efforts for the healthy preservation of our racial inheritance. . . To a greater extent than formerly it will make the object of its efforts life in its natural structures: . . . education to become a German with the basic qualities this connotes of the heroic, the warlike, the priority given to honour and above all the readiness to sacrifice oneself for the community. It is thus glad to serve national political education: in commitment to one's homeland, people and State it sees an obligation that ultimately rests on religious foundations' (p. 164). As early as 1934 a prelate had been quite clear and unambiguous in a pastoral letter: 'This is the basic attitude of the German Catholic towards the new State—loyalty to the State is loyalty to God.' One example of the expression given to this basic attitude is to be found in a fourth verse added to the hymn *Grosser Gott, wir loben dich* in the 1939 Catholic military hymnal: 'Wherever our standards wave, on land or on sea, let loyalty stand guard and be our weapon and bulwark. The watchword is to be: "Loyal to the Führer, the people and the nation." ' Another hymn, *Fest soll mein Taufbund immer steh'n*, also acquired and additional verse: 'I shall maintain what in solemn oath I have sworn to God: to serve the *Volk* and the authorities loyally till death. I shall not waver or despair but love honour and duty, so help me God.'

2. MILITARY CHAPLAINS AS A MEANS TO POLITICAL ENDS

Without previous discussion with the Church authorities the Army Supreme Command issued in August 1939 'Instructions on pastoral care in the services' which

31

included general statements on the nature and tasks of the service chaplaincies alongside many detailed prescriptions. According to the general experience of war 'an army's spiritual strength is its best weapon'. But this strength was primarily derived from a firm faith. 'The pastoral work of military chaplains is thus an important means for strengthening the army's offensive effectiveness.' Hence its primary task was 'to serve the fighting troops'. Someone who understands and appreciated his service as a soldier to the fatherland and his commitment as a charge laid on him by God, who trusted in God and looked forward to eternal life, 'can endure steadfastly, fight bravely and die courageously'.

These ideas, nourished by the traditional conception of the faith, by apologetics and by the sermons delivered in earlier wars, was taken up by military chaplains and used to legitimate their activity against those who rejected the system of military chaplains and wanted to end it. There is no doubt that many priests regarded these arguments as well-founded, took them seriously and believed them.

Up till the end of the war the military chaplaincies counted as an official department of the Armed Forces. The most important document for the Wehrmacht leadership's policy in this regard, the *Guidelines for Military Chaplaincies* published in May 1942, is quite explicit. Article 1 states: 'The victorious outcome of the National Socialist fight for freedom is decisive for the future of the German national community and thus for the future of every individual German. Pastoral work in the *Wehrmacht* must take this fact unequivocally into account.' Right from the beginning of the war and particularly after the attack on the Soviet Union it was known that the Nazi Party looked for a stronger commitment from the churches than they were ready to give. This expectation was now spelled out quite openly with regard to military chaplaincies in a way that made it tantamount to an ultimatum.

3. WHAT THE CHURCH HAD TO SAY DURING THE WAR

(a) Statements by German bishops

Neither in German society as a whole nor within the churches did the initial reaction to the outbreak of war in 1939 begin to resemble that which greeted the outbreak of war in 1914, even among those who had greeted Hitler's temporary successes in foreign affairs more or less enthusiastically. Enthusiasm is not in fact to be found in any pastoral letter by a diocesan bishop, but the exhortation to soldiers and faithful to do their duty was all the more frequent and persistent. The basic ideas expressed by the German bishops in their joint statement of September 1939 recur in practically all the pastorals by individual bishops: 'In this decisive hour we urge and exhort our Catholic soldiers to do their duty in obedience towards the Führer, ready to sacrifice themselves and committing their entire personality. We summon the faithful people to ardent prayer that God's providence may guide the war that has broken out to a success and peace rich in blessings for our fatherland and our people . . . (*Vaterland and Volk*).'[1]

Pastoral letters by numerous diocesan bishops include appeals like: 'Fulfil your duty to your Führer, your people and your fatherland', 'May God be with all who take on themselves the hard task of war and give their courage and strength to fight victoriously for their dear fatherland or bravely to die for it', or even: 'Following Christ means risking one's own life for the deliverance of our people and nation.'[2] It is difficult to understand these statements by German bishops as other than a recognition of the justice of the war. That meant, according to the traditional teaching, that Catholics were bound in conscience to loyalty to Hitler. But anyone who recognised Hitler's war as just was giving at least partial legitimation to the hostile stereotypes fixed in people's consciousness by Nazi propaganda. By talking about 'the war that has been forced on us' (Gröber)[3] one could suggest the idea of innocent, peaceloving Germany and its enemies greedy for war. One could see in the war that had just begun a kind of continuation of the First World War, 'ostensibly ended in 1919 by a peace imposed by force' (von Galen),[4] and thus conjure up earlier pictures of Germany surrounded by envious enemies. For a later generation it remains difficult to understand how in many statements the German bishops went on demanding doing one's duty to the fatherland, being ready to sacrifice oneself, loyalty and obedience. But at the same time one must recognise that the examples cited from Gröber and von Galen represent exceptions. The bishops were extremely reticent in interpreting the war up until the attack on the Soviet Union, which was presented as a 'struggle against Godless Bolshevism'.

Among all the bishops it was only Bishop Preysing of Berlin who had nothing to say about the 'war for the fatherland'. He exhorted Catholics and soldiers to be ready at any moment to face their God.

The general tone of what the bishops had to say about the war can be summed up as follows: they were upset and worried about the war that had broken out but, in keeping with traditional Catholic teaching about people's duties to the lawful authorities and wanting to maintain patriotic solidarity, they appealed seriously and with reticence for people to do their duty and stand firm. From the middle of 1940 traces can be found of a certain fervour which may be based on pride in the achievements of German soldiers but which may also in part be conditioned by the demands of the Ministry of Propaganda for greater commitment. Perhaps a part was played here and there by the idea of being able favourably to influence the possible victor with regard to the period after the war. The attitudes the bishops took to the war and the statements they made cannot be reduced to a single factor, since on this question, too, the episcopate was divided and individual bishops changed their positions as the war progressed. In this way it is not possible either to talk of the German bishops' 'unreserved support of the German war aims' or to say that 'the bishops and Catholics never prayed for the victory of the Third Reich but only for a just peace'.

(b) The military bishop Franz Justus Rarkowski (1873-1950)

The forty-one texts extant from the pen of the bishop-in-ordinary to the German Armed Forces go far beyond the statements of the diocesan bishops. Thus the bishop concluded his Lenten pastoral of 16 January 1940 with the 'Easter wish' that 'the German soul may prove itself victorious in this struggle that has been forced upon it and achieve a peace that will give a new countenance to tired Europe and guarantee our people peace, security and betterment'.[5] A pastoral sent to all military chaplains ended: 'It is now your task, as participants in this current difficult and decisive passage of arms under the command of our supreme commander, to co-operate with all your power by your selfless commitment to bringing about a victorious peace that will give our nation that position among the countries of Europe to which according to God's creative will it can lay an intrinsic claim' (15 June 1940). The pastoral that Rarkowski wrote at the end of the first year of the war is soaked in the terminology and fervour of Nazi propaganda to an extent hardly paralleled by any other of his writings. In this it is a question of fighting for survival 'against the arrogant presumption of rich nations which in their blindness thought they could obliterate us and trample us underfoot'. In this the war is described as 'unavoidable'. In this one can also read: 'It is one of the mysteries of war that it gives human life a form of existence raised to the highest point. . . .' Christian faith was not 'a component part of your spiritual and moral rearmament' but also made it clear 'that military service as commitment on behalf of the community, the nation and the country is not only a sublime human calling, not only a giving of oneself to the supreme values of the nation, but also a genuinely Christian task and action according to the example and words of Christ' (1 September 1940). In the Lenten pastoral of 2 February 1941 Good Friday and the 'German passion', the 'sepulchre of a cruel peace treaty' (Versailles), are juxtaposed, just as are Easter morning and 'the Easter light of our resurrection as a people and a nation'. Tied up with this is a glorification of German history ('the nation that is Europe's heart', 'our ancestors were immortals', 'German achievement to the ends of the earth') which Rarkowski was concerned to expound for his soldiers, these young men who were taking the world by storm, on the basis of 'eternity'. For the military bishop the war against the Soviet Union counted as a 'European crusade' and as a contribution 'for the entire world of European culture against the barbarians of Bolshevism' (24 July 1941) with the goal of eradicating 'Bolshevism from history for all time'.

(c) Sermon outlines for military chaplains

Between 1940 and 1944 the Church's War Aid, a department of German Caritas, produced twenty-nine series of sermon outlines which were distributed to some 2,000 priests. Apart from the first issues each series comprised about thirty pages.[6] Among these sermons for soldiers two themes are of importance in this context: the meaning of the war on the one hand and the soldier's moral attitude to the war on the other. The attempt to interpret what was happening in the war included, alongside attempts at a general explanation in terms of morality or intellectual history, interpretations of the war as Germany's struggle for its alleged rights and above all as the defence of Western culture against Bolshevism: in particular soldiers were reminded of the close links between the Christian and the military attitude to life as well as the obligation to loyalty brought about by the oath of allegiance and the significance of the soldier's death. The love of one's country demanded by morality was love of Germany in this war that was 'our nation's fight for freedom' (XVII: 28). 'For us, our country is sacred. For it we are gladly willing to sacrifice our youth, our health and our vitality, even in the front line. For us the fatherland is sacred. We honour God's holy will in our Germanity. The honour of our country is our honour, its freedom is our freedom, its rights are our rights, its sacrifice is our sacrifice. Christ, too, loved his native land, and loved it so much that he gave his life for it. Thus it is right and in keeping with God's spirit that we should be penetrated by a profound and incomparable love of our fatherland' (IX: 10). From time to time what finds expression is how little in the past people had come to terms with the challenges inseparable from a democracy, how much they remained imprisoned in authoritarian ways of thought, and the extent to which the present was misunderstood. Thus one outline begins by explicitly analysing the 'period of our fatherland's external servitude after the collapse of the Red Revolution of 1918' and the 'false freedom' proclaimed in those years. It goes on: 'These times are, thank God, past, my friends, and in the new Germany and its wealth of ideas the real meaning of real freedom has come into its own once again. . . . And so it is no accident that in our nation's fight for freedom which ultimately will also make the world inwardly free our soldiers should bear the motto "God with us" on their belt-buckles—as Catholic soldiers to accomplish this task with Him and under Him' (XIX: 15-16).

When Germany's mission is seen in these terms the conviction that God's blessing rests on Germany is a necessary consequence, especially since the initial victories seemed to confirm this conclusion: 'The time must demand hard things of you, and heroic deeds will be done by you. But blessing must rest on this heroism of the achievements of our incomparably proud army. All your exertions, all your courage, all your sacrifice in the service of our beloved German land and people will one day stand inscribed in the golden book of life' (XII: 9). Just as in the statements of the Propaganda Ministry, so too in these sermons the war was called 'the casting of the bell of the Germans and thus of the European future'; one saw how 'the field of a past age was forcefully broken up' by the war which was claimed to be 'the most vital collaborator in this gigantic work' that served 'the emergence of a new world' (XII: 21).

The fight against the Soviet Union gave the war a new dimension. Now it was no longer a question of simply referring to the German people's right to life and its fight for freedom. There was an almost immediate latching on to previous Church statements about Bolshevism, and it was explained 'what a people without religion is as it vegetates in apathetic gloom' (XII: 23). The mere fact that in the Soviet Union an open struggle was being conducted against Christianity and religion was enough for some preachers to legitimate Hitler's war, to give it a religious dedication and beyond this to present Germany as the champion of Christianity. The fight against 'the most terrible enemy of the Christian name on European soil for nearly two thousand years' occasionally led to ideas of a crusade and to references to the German mission in history. The suspicion is well-founded that remarks about Bolshevism and talk of the 'Christian face of Germany' and of Europe contained a deliberate if subliminal criticism of the philosophy and policies of Nazism, and it was a criticism that was understood as such by many people. But that cannot abolish the fact that even in the Church's proclamation German aggression was at least indirectly represented as justified and that the feelings of German superiority that were already present in overabundance were strengthened still more and given a religious embellishment.

4. PATRIOTISM AS A FORM OF SELF-DEFENCE?

To understand these statements we should not forget the enormous mass of propaganda which the party used in order to drum into the collective German consciousness the idea that Christianity and the Church were alien to the German nature. Christianity was a slave religion for weaklings and those unfit for life, the Church was an institution hostile to everything German, bishops and priests were currently speculators and led immoral lives: all this proclaimed loudly and continuously could not be without its effect, particularly on young people. Catholic writing from that period is to a great extent moulded by the concern to refute and reject these and other claims, reproaches and attacks. If in those years a series of books was published in which the relationship of Christianity to Germanity is gone into and German history is described as decisively marked by the Christian message, in which the heroic character of Christianity is prominent, and loyalty to one's native land, people and nation is stressed as an important element of the Christian view of morality, then statements of this kind should not simply be seen as the expression of a readiness to conform but rather as attempts at self-defence against massive propaganda.[7] It is difficult to reproach those who presumed to go on writing after 1933 with defending themselves against calumnies and unfounded attacks. It is of course another question whether in this people were always politically, educationally and theologically prudent and irreproachable enough and whether the emphasis on what the Church and the new State had in common, even during the first years of the war, did not erase outlines where a clear distinction should have been drawn.

5. CRITICISM WITHIN THE CHURCH

The military chaplain Joseph Perau entered in his diary for 13 June 1940: 'Some young seminarians are taking enthusiastically to the life of a soldier. They want to show that they, too, are national. The continual slanders of propaganda have created something like an inferiority complex.'[8]

That even the pope was not without anxiety with regard to the patriotic attitude of priests called up for military service can be deduced from his letter to Archbishop Gröber of 1 March 1942. Assuring the archbishop of his prayers for priests and seminarians called up for military service, he expressed the wish that among other things they might 'keep themselves free from erroneous ideas', what he seemed to be suggesting was the need for 'excessive national enthusiasm' to be held in check by 'right ideas'.[9] The pope was not imagining things, even if national enthusiasm was a long way from reaching the degree of 1914. Many priests and even bishops had hoped that among the demands of war the measures aimed against the Church would be removed. But despite the Church's efforts to prove its loyalty to the fatherland the aggressive policy towards the Church was, after a short pause, continued. The former vicar general of the Armed Forces, Mgr Werthmann, noted in a private memorandum on 3 July 1945: 'The persecution of the Church that not only continued during the war but to some extent increased, the closing of religious houses and schools, the confiscation of Church property, the removal of priests to Dachau, the ban on pastoral letters, the prohibition of any paper allowance for religious books, catechisms and hymn books could only have an unfavourable effect on our military chaplains at the fronts. This kind of news was only too likely to encourage passive resistance. As a result a large proportion of chaplains distanced themselves more and more from any kind of emphasis on motives of patriotism and confined themselves to preaching the truths of the faith.' If these observations are correct, then it was less an awareness of the wrongness of Hitler's war than the realisation that a change in the system's attitude towards the Catholic Church could not even be brought about by the sacrifice of its own life that led to a distancing from 'emphasis on motives of patriotism'.

6. THE POWER OF 'GHOSTS'

A few weeks after the Second World War ended the former vicar general of the Armed Forces jotted down in his detention these thoughts in which he apostrophised his dead comrades: 'You went wrong just as we did. You fulfilled your duty as soldiers for ghosts whose images were used to delude you. But you went wrong in the best of good faith and with pure intentions. We on the other hand must still be purified, and this has not been done with the realisation that has dawned on us over a few days and weeks. . . .' (28 June 1945). Here we can no longer go into the question why so many people's thinking and judgment was influenced so strongly by the categories of natural law and by patriotic concern and why the word of the Gospel availed so little towards the discernment of spirits and the banishment of 'ghosts'. In conclusion we must merely point out with dismay that even in our own day Christians and bishops became the patriotic auxiliaries of whichever nation they belonged to during a senseless war for a few rocks in the South Atlantic. The power of ghosts has not yet been broken.

Translated by Robert Nowell

Notes

1. Quoted from F. Strobel *Christliche Bewährung. Dokumente des Widerstandes der katholischen Kirche in Deutschland 1939-1945* (Olten 1946) p. 268.

2. *Seelsorge und kirchliche Verwaltung im Krieg. Gesetze, Verfügungen und Richtlinien* ed K. Hotmann (Freiburg-im-Breisgau 1940) pp. 3 and 7; Strobel, in the work cited in note 1, p. 59.

3. Lenten pastoral of Archbishop Gröber, quoted by Strobel, in the work cited in note 1, p. 59.

4. Bishop von Galen, quoted by G. C. Zahn *Die deutschen Katholiken und Hitlers Kriege* (Graz and Cologne 1965) p. 134.

5. The pastoral letters of Bishop Rarkowski are to be found in the archives of the Catholic Military Ordinariate, Bonn, as are the issues of the *Verordnungsblatt des katholischen Feldbischofs der Wehrmacht*.

6. The central archives of the German Caritasverband have series I-XX of these sermons filed under 370, 17 (2) and series XXI-XXIX under 370, 17 (3). They are cited by series number and page.

7. See K. Speckner *Die Wächter der Kirche* (Munich 1934); A. Aich *Im Dienste zweier Könige* (Breslau 1937); T. Bogler *Der Glaube von Gestern und Morgen* (Cologne 1939); J. Walterscheid *Deutsche Heilige* (Munich 1934).

8. J. Perau *Priester im Heere Hitlers* (Essen [2]1963) p.8.

9. B. Schneider *Die Briefe Pius XII. an die deutschen Bischöfe 1939-1944* (Mainz 1966) note 1-1.

Miguel D'Escoto

Thoughts on the Church Based on the Nicaraguan Experience

1. INTRODUCTION

ALTHOUGH I feel very close to the work of professional theologians, I am not one myself; I am, however, a Christian and a priest who tries to live his faith in Christ the liberator. And we all know that it is impossible to live something without translating it to the level of at least a certain degree of thought. Going back over one's experience in this way enriches it and gives it new impetus. My life, in common with that of many of my readers, has led me to live and think my faith in the bosom of a poor people struggling to liberate itself. It has also led me through this process in the company of many who do not call themselves Christians, but who in practice carry out the evangelical counsels to the ultimate degree. I owe much in my life to their form of witness.

As I said, I am not a professional theologian, but surely theology is only reflection on Christian life? If it is, then in its broadest and first sense, it is the task of all Christians. Which is why someone once said that it is too important to be left to theologians. . . .

The experience on which these thoughts are based is that of a poor country, that of a people which, like so many others in the Third World, has been through a situation of exploitation and deprivation, while at the same time struggling and dying to set itself free. In Nicaragua, which is the specific experience of which I want to speak, the people have given their lives to combat the death brought by hunger, disease and repression. We have been through—still are going through—hard times, but times full of hope; sorrowing times, but nevertheless filled with a deep joy; times of rejection and bereavement, but also of re-building. The main point is that this is not the experience of a few isolated individuals, but of a whole people together. The Nicaraguan experience is marked by its popular, collective, mass character. Much has been written about the Christian participation in the national liberation struggle in Nicaragua; it is therefore important to point out that the most meaningful participation was that of the whole people: Christians took part because our struggle was a popular process and the people are Christian. The struggle was not centred on minorities, but on its base in the heart of the whole people.

The experience of the Nicaraguan people has been that of an exploited people struggling to liberate itself, but also that of a Christian people living its faith in the heart of the struggle, and singing its faith in the God of the poor at masses in the countryside. And is this not proclaiming the kingdom of God, the kingdom of justice and life? Is this not beginning to forge, through Christian communities, a Church that can be a sign of the presence of the kingdom in history?

There is here, it seems to me, and I would like to suggest to you, a way forward for an ecclesiology which is not limited to saying what the Church of Jesus Christ should be, but which is the result of reflecting on what is being done, what is being built (re-built, in the case of Nicaragua) in history. So it is not an abstract and ingenuous 'should be', but a demanding and realistic 'is'.

2. THE EXPERIENCE OF A PEOPLE

It is impossible to encapsulate all the richness of a people's experience in a few sentences, the more so as this experience is characterised by process, movement, newness. Nevertheless, let me try to pick out a few of its salient characteristics which seem relevant to these reflections.

(a) A paschal joy

One of the most striking impressions made by the people of Nicaragua is the joy they showed in the struggle recently, and show in the process of reconstruction now—even at the present time when we are having to prepare to defend our gains and our dignity as a free people against the threats of invasion from those who seek to re-impose their domination from outside. This is not a subjective view; this joy is deeply ingrained in the faces of the people, expresses itself in their songs and above all in the energy they are putting into the rebuilding of a country ground down by tyranny, devastated by war, threatened by the enemy. This is no casual joy, but the result of having passed through suffering and death, together with the knowledge that having gone through this experience, we are beginning to overcome the suffering produced by an unjust economic system, and the death brought about by exploitation and repression.

This joy shows itself in a hope which allows us to look the future squarely in the face. The oppressor only has a past to look back on and so kills in an effort to hold history back. Only the poor have a future. The rich will be sent empty away, while the hands of the poor are full of history, as Mary, mother of the Saviour and daughter of her people, tells us.

The Church, the assembly convened by Jesus Christ, cannot turn its back on this joy of the poor people of Latin America. More than this, it must feed on it, its pulse must beat with these people. This is harder than it might appear at first sight. The Church's past is full of complicities, deliberate or otherwise, with the forces of oppression, and this has often prevented the Church from recognising itself in the subversive joy of a people fighting for a worthy human life. And yet the Church professes its faith in the resurrection, in a life that conquers death and confounds those who deal in death. But still the Church has so often been, alas, far from the efforts of those struggling to free themselves from oppression, not knowing how to live with them and with their struggles and their hopes.

By behaving in this way, is the Church not denying itself as the Church of Christ present in the poor of this world, in those in whom Puebla tells us we should recognise 'the suffering features of Christ the Lord' (n. 31)? If it is, then it is living—or rather, which is worse and shocking to any true Christian, dying—on the fringes of the Gospel, the Good News which it must proclaim and which at the same time judges it. But happily, there are throughout this continent Christian communities that have rooted themselves in the people and their struggle and who are celebrating the passage from death to life in the joy of the poor. Many Christians in Nicaragua have learnt that it is

Davidson College Library

impossible to believe without fighting for justice. So a Church is constantly being born from the faith and hope of the poor. We can all benefit from reflecting on these facts and nourishing ourselves on this hope.

(b) Makers of history

Throughout their history, the poor people of Nicaragua, like those of the rest of Latin America, have been deprived not only of the fruits of their labour, but of their lives, their freedom and their country. But there are also points at which this historical process is broken, times when the oppressed rise up and claim their rights. In Nicaragua the best expression of this protest was the time marked by the outstanding figure of the 'general of the free', Augusto César Sandino, and, following him, Carlos Fonseca Amador and so many others who ploughed a deep furrow in the history of my country and sowed a seed that the Somoza regime tried in vain to root out. But the seed had taken root in land watered by the blood of the poor, and there it flourished and grew till it produced the harvest we are reaping now.

It forced the genocidal tyrant to flee. People gave their lives for this freedom, feeling themselves masters of their own country for the first time in history, not because someone else had granted it to them, but because they had won it, with arms in their hands and hope in their hearts. This struggle to take history into one's own hands is one of the marks of the experience of the people of Nicaragua and also of the poor people of the rest of the continent. It is a long day's struggle, with some premature darkenings, but also with glowing dawns that summon us to work under the sun.

These people, making their own history, call into question and at the same time enrich our understanding of the Church. The people of God will henceforth be made up of men and women ever more conscious of their right to life, freedom and justice. If the Christian message as proclaimed fails to take this growing maturity of the people into account, it will be relegated to the private, individual sphere, remaining on the sidelines of history. The Church often feels awkward in its relationship with these efforts at national liberation. Its conscious and unconscious links with the world against which the poor fight are stronger than it realises. This makes it feel put out, alienated, uncertain and sometimes even hostile to these processes. There are historical cases in which the Church—mainly in its institutional aspect—has had, and still sometimes has, the same reactions as the dominating classes and has contributed to defending their interests. At other times it has echoed the fears and plaints of the middle classes who see their privileges threatened by these triumphant popular uprisings, privileges which they consider to be theirs as of right; as if there could be a right to exploit, deceive and despoil the poor.

When this happens, I do not think we can talk simply of a failure to appreciate the situation correctly, or of individual errors. I would say that it stems rather from a particular way of regarding the Church and its role in history, in which the poor with their lives, struggles and aspirations, simply do not figure. For their presence to become a reality we need an exodus to a land still foreign to the Church of today: the land of the poor. Making their world ours means being converted to the great poor and oppressed majorities of this world, to those with whom we try organically to link our reflections on faith in Jesus Christ the liberator.

Puebla has called the Latin American Church to such a conversion: 'To live out and proclaim the requirement of Christian poverty, the Church must re-examine its structures and the life of its members . . . with the goal of effective conversion in mind' (n. 1157). For such a call to have been made possible means that the process has already begun in the actual life of the continent. The numbers of Christians and Christian communities who have linked their fate to that of the poor is in fact constantly growing;

Davidson College Library

these people are breaking with the old man and setting out on untrodden paths towards the making of the new man.

But the heart of the matter is that this is basically a question of *spirituality*. This classical term is perhaps largely misunderstood today. In fact, to talk about spirituality means simply to talk about a way of being Christian. We need to realise that fidelity to the Gospel today involves a break with our familiar known world, in which the Church has bought peace at the cost of forgetting the Gospel imperatives. As Christians who are proclaiming and building up the kingdom, we cannot but rebel against such a situation. But breaking away is only one side of the coin; the other is giving oneself daringly and courageously to the cause of the poor, in the certainty that theirs is the cause of Christ.

(c) Solidarity in struggle

Tyrants tend to divide and fragment the poor, to make them believe that they are only isolated individuals and not a social class, a culture, a race. They try to make them think that each one of them can and should break out of their situation of poverty individually, if necessary treading on the backs of their class and race brothers to do so. This individualistic mentality is a mark of the ruling classes, who do not recognise friends, only potential allies who will help them to maintain their privileges.

One of the most impressive things about the Nicaraguan revolution has been the growth of solidarity and unity: unity of the people, of the workers, peasants, villagers and students, a unity of the masses forged by the 'United People Movement', a unity of the whole people with their vanguard the FSLN (Sandinista Front for National Liberation), a unity between all tendencies within the Front. This unity of the people has been strong enough to persuade many of the middle classes who were opposed to Somoza, to draw most young people into the movement, and to encourage women to play an outstanding part. It has also been strong enough to win international support, which shook the Organisation of American States and regional groupings on the continent. Nicaragua was thus able, at the height of the struggle, to unite most countries of Latin America against Somoza, leaving the United States isolated.

This unity and solidarity have been the strength of the revolutionary process which has made the Nicaraguan one people, a people determined to make itself present in history, from which the dictator had tried to make it disappear, a people proud of its own values. This solidarity is at once the cause and the effect of the revolutionary struggle. We also experience it as the reality of the oppressed of the Third World throughout the length and breadth of Latin America. We have experienced it in war, and we shall go on experiencing it in reconstruction. Their generosity in the struggle, the blood this exploited Christian people has shed, have produced a qualitative leap forward in human nature. This step has been taken in concrete action and could not have been produced by a preaching devoid of acts of solidarity. The Church will not be the assembly convoked by the word of Jesus if it does not have, like the Samaritan on the road to Jericho, the courage to leave the well-trodden track, to care for the wounded man, the beaten-up, robbed people. Only then will the Church realise that only by drawing near to, acting in solidarity with the poor and the oppressed, can it become a neighbour to them and make this people its neighbour.

Here I should like to quote from the important pastoral letter issued by the bishops of Nicaragua in November 1979 (six months after the success of the revolution): 'Today in our country we are living through an exceptional opportunity for witnessing and proclaiming the kingdom of God. It would be a serious infidelity to the Gospel if, out of fear and resentment, or the insecurity some feel in any process of radical social change, or a wish to defend small or large individual interests, we were to allow this moment to pass by, a moment in which we are called on to put into action that preferential option

D

for the poor, as required both by Pope John Paul II and by the Episcopal Conference at Puebla.' And they went on to spell out clearly what this opportunity means for the life of the Church: 'This option requires that we abandon old ways of thinking and behaving: it requires a deep conversion of ourselves as Church. In effect, the day the Church ceases to present itself to the world as poor and on the side of the poor, it will betray its divine founder and the proclamation of the kingdom of God. Never has it been as urgent to put this preferential option for the poor into practice with conviction as it is now in the present situation of Nicaragua.'

To avoid any misunderstanding about the identity of the poor referred to, the bishops went on: 'The poor Jesus speaks of, whom he surrounded himself with, are real poor people, genuinely poor, hungry, afflicted, oppressed; they are all those of whom no account is taken in the organisation of society and who are rejected by society. It was on the basis of this solidarity with the poor that Jesus proclaimed the Father's love for every human being, and faced his suffering, persecution and death.'

This term 'solidarity', so deeply rooted in our people and of such significance in Latin America in the past few years, was taken up by John Paul II in his latest encyclical, *Laborem Exercens*. In this, speaking of the solidarity needed with workers' movements in defence of their rights, the pope clearly says of the Church: 'The Church is fully committed to this cause, considering it its mission and service as proof of its fidelity to Christ, in order to be truly the "Church of the poor" ' (n. 8). It is this commitment that proves its fidelity to the Lord. Only in this way can John XXII's intuition, formulated exactly twenty years ago, that the Church must be a Church of the poor, be actualised. The Nicaraguan experience, and that of so many other people who are our brothers, shows that being a disciple of Jesus today means being ready to face death in order to give life to those robbed and assassinated by a system of exploitation.

3. SOME CONSEQUENCES

The above outline of the characteristics of the joy of a people being makers of their own history and solidarity in struggle is meant to show that it is not possible to separate building up the Church from making a history of freedom and justice. Separating them would mean failing to see the connection between the Church and the kingdom, the poor and the God of the Bible. A short while ago, some members of the basic communities wrote to John Paul II: 'We know that the Church, in all times and in all countries, has always had similar tensions. You are calling us to unity, and we want to heed your call. We know that through looking at Jesus, listening to his word and following his way, we will all, together with our bishops, discover that God wants us to work in unity for the good of the poorest. You have often repeated that the Church is the Church of the poor, because they are the chosen ones of God. We are going to unite in this commitment to the poor and to justice and peace' (letter of 15 August 1982).

This means that the characteristics I outlined are not merely interesting historical facts to be observed with sympathy. They are in my view—and this is what matters to us here—ecclesiological questions, challenges to the action and very being of the Church. How, in effect, can the Church be 'a kind of sacrament or sign of intimate union with God, and of the unity of all mankind' (LG, 1) without taking account of and denouncing everything that destroys that union? How can we be followers of Jesus without taking upon ourselves the efforts of the poor to make that union a historical reality?

Understanding the kingdom of God and believing in the kingdom of God means living in solidarity with the oppressed poor of this world. This is the practical and theoretical *locus* of ecclesiology. The Church is both experienced and thought about in this relationship with the poor. The kingdom it proclaims is made present in a history in which the poor are fighting for their most elementary rights. The historical place where we meet Jesus is where we stand in the process of liberation.

At the same time this kingdom-poor relationship challenges the Church and judges its presence in the world. Its task is to serve Christ who told us that we would meet him in our brothers in need. So the Church is continually reborn from the poor and the oppressed, that is from what is deepest and most distinctive in it: its faith in the Lord. This is what we mean by a Church of the poor; this is what we are trying to build in Nicaragua within a process of liberation.

The first thing I have tried to show is our modest contribution, based on our revolutionary experience, to building up an ecclesiology which explains the hope found in the Popular Christian Communities. I hope readers of this review will reflect on our experience; our triumph in revolution has made us progress, but that does not mean we have the whole truth. We should like our conclusions to be a contribution to the whole Church in Latin America, and to take account of the struggles and the thoughts of all. We do not want to separate Nicaragua from the movements of liberation and ecclesial renewal throughout Latin America and the rest of the Third World. We have something to give, and an awful lot to learn.

Our union in liberation and our hope experienced and celebrated in a Church rising up in the midst of the people's struggle through the power of the Holy Spirit must be translated, nevertheless, into specific terms. We have overthrown Somoza, but we have still not overcome all he stands for and its supporters at home and overseas. Furthermore we still have to rebuild our country, devastated by tyranny, earthquake and war, and now threatened by mercenaries and the forces of reaction. The most reactionary elements of United States policy are even now on the lookout, waiting for the best moment to destroy us. We need the solidarity of all the peoples of Latin America and the rest of the world: economic and political solidarity, solidarity to fight counter-revolution, solidarity to break the blockade and isolation to which some would like to subject us, and to ward off the invasion we are threatened with.

We trust only in the solidarity of the poor, and we are convinced that the actions of committed Christians will be decisive in bringing about this broad movement of solidarity across this continent and the world. It is in such struggles that we Christians, throughout the length and breadth of this continent, are proclaiming our faith and hope in the God who frees. Celebrating this faith and hope is not something inherited from our religious upbringing; this celebration of the death and resurrection of Christ is a continuing *novelty*, sustained today by the generous sacrifice of those 'dead who never die' as we call them in Nicaragua, because like Christ they died for love and for the liberation of their people.

The victory of 19 July 1979 is only a beginning. I should like to call on everyone in his place of struggle and all of us together to complete our process of liberation, in Nicaragua today and, sooner rather than later, throughout our 'Great Country' of Latin America. There, as in Europe in the early centuries, a Church is growing nourished by the blood of martyrs. The best known and most meaningful case is Mgr Romero in El Salvador, but every day there are anonymous witnesses who suffer for the justice and freedom of their people, inspired by a deep faith in the Lord. Their death saddens us because of the huge human cost it represents, but at the same time it fills us with hope.

Translated by Paul Burns

Joseph Comblin

War and the Right of Self-Defence

IN ANCIENT times, Rome was able to conquer and subjugate sixty different peoples, solely by means of wars of self-defence, which were therefore just wars. By a skilful strategy of alliances and provocative measures, Rome always arranged things in such a way that the peoples she wished to conquer put themselves in the wrong in the first instance. She then intervened to avenge the right and to re-establish justice.

This example shows clearly the extent to which the role of morality is adventitious and superficial where war is concerned. Moreover, in every war the rival parties always invoke just motives, and each one always considers itself as the victim forced to defend its rights. There are never any wars which are not just wars on both sides, at least in the opinion of the combatants. States always make war to defend justice. This is why the moral doctrine of the just war is so ineffectual.

Despite this, is it not still possible for morality to exercise some measure of influence on war, either to prevent it, to bring it to an end, to limit or to moderate it? At first sight, the experience of history has not been very encouraging. However, if one does not expect morality to produce either radical reversals of policy or absolute purity of conduct, it is not impossible to see, even in recent events, that the moral reactions of individuals or groups, especially when these reactions are supported by churches, can have a certain effect. The influence of the moral factor is generally difficult to detect. It never acts alone. Other factors may operate in the same direction. How may one discern, for example, in the campaigns in the United States from 1967 onwards against the war in Vietnam, how much influence was exerted by moral feeling and how much by business circles moved by economic considerations? It is probable that, on its own, morality is never powerful enough to modify the course of events or to inspire changes in the political will of nations. But the moral factor can have an influence when it happens to be supported by other factors which, on their own, would be just as incapable of imposing a decision.

1. THE IDEOLOGIES AND THE REALITY OF WAR

The moral sense may act first of all in furthering the clear comprehension of war. Understanding is not outside the sphere of morality. The understanding of war is now, as in the past, clouded by ideologies. The attempt to distinguish between the ideology

44

and the reality of war can in itself be a contribution to peace, since the ideological view may tend to have recourse to war more readily or enthusiastically.

At the present time there are two great ideologies of war, the Marxist-Leninist and the American. In addition to these two there are, in the Third World, fragmentary attempts to formulate an independent ideology.

According to the Soviet ideology, which claims to be Marxist-Leninist, war is always, in the final analysis, linked to the class struggle, and thus to imperialism. War results from the aggressive policies of American imperialism. The policy of the Soviet Union is essentially peaceful. Despite the aggressiveness of American imperialism, war is not inevitable, however, for 'the revolutionary struggle for the dictatorship of the proletariat includes the exertion of overt political pressure on the exploiters; it does not necessarily involve armed struggle'.[1]

The American ideology is included in the 'strategy' of the military academies of the USA and its satellites, especially in the Third World. It is based first of all on the experience of Munich and on the doctrine of total war first expounded by Ludendorff.[2]

The Munich experience teaches the necessity of dissuading any aggressive power imbued with a desire for world conquest. At the present time, the Soviet Union is that power. There is no doubt that it aims to conquer the world and takes advantage of every opportunity to further that aim. Behind all the conflicts in the modern world lurks this Soviet desire for conquest. This is, in particular, the source of the revolutionary wars and the wars of national liberation in the Third World.

This brings us to the second element of this ideology, that of total war. As a result of the new weapons and the change in revolutions, war has become total. Henceforth it embraces military, political, economic and ideological activities. Clausewitz's formula is reversed: it is politics which is the continuation of war by every means. Faced with the permanent presence of the enemy through subversion in all its forms, the State is always in a situation of virtual war. The recourse to arms is no longer a qualitative change.

This ideology tends to stimulate military action. In effect, it tends to exaggerate the threat posed by the enemy and therefore to encourage preventive military action. The domino theory applied formerly in South-East Asia and currently in Central America is one example of this. In addition, it facilitates recourse to arms in situations where other means might be sufficient. There seems to be no doubt that American bellicosity since the end of the Second World War has been encouraged by the ideology of the military.

In the Third World, the ideology according to which imperialism, whether it be the vestiges of the declining imperialism of France or Great Britain, American imperialism, or even, for some observers, Soviet imperialism, lies behind every military action, is usually quite favourably received. This view easily reassures the consciences of adventurist heads of State or dictators playing the part of the Sorcerer's Apprentice. The struggle against imperialism justifies everything (for example the war between Iraq and Iran, or Argentina's war for the Falklands, or the wars in Ethiopia or Chad). Naturally, in today's world, it is difficult for anything to occur without the Great Powers being involved. Yet this is no reason to make them the universal explanation. In reality, to demystify the ideologies is in itself to work for peace.

2. THE LOGIC OF WAR

There are naïve forms of pacifism which ignore the logic of war. Some believe that for the peoples of the world to express their determination to reject war would be enough to make war impossible. It is not difficult to call upon experience or reason to show that declarations of a refusal to fight can themselves provoke a war. One cannot act directly upon war, since it is part of an overall structure and it obeys its own logic.

One cannot act upon war except by acting on the structure as a whole. War has its own rationality and to influence it one must enter into that rationality.

War is not simply the unleashing of aggression or violence. War is a form of violence which is organised and limited. It is only possible if it is limited. Nuclear war was impossible so long as it was seen as unlimited. Now that we know that a limited nuclear war is possible, it enters the realm of the possible.

War is not made by peoples with their aggressive instincts or their individual violence. It is States which make war, using armed forces which are institutionalised and professionally trained. The violence of the civilian population plays no part in this. A people may be gentle and peaceable, but may be led by a warmongering State apparatus. War is the business of States and armies.

Clausewitz's dictum must be kept in mind:[3] war is the continuation of politics by other means, that is, by military action.

War serves political ends. It is the State which determines its political ends. Peoples and their moral conscience can only affect war in so far as they can intervene to determine the political goals of the State. We live at present within a world order composed of individual States,[4] of which the first principle is national sovereignty. So long as this principle remains in force, it will be impossible to eliminate war from international relations, for the sovereign nation does not admit any authority above itself able to enforce justice. The sovereign State defines, for itself alone, its own rights and therefore what constitutes political justice. In addition, the State reserves to itself the exclusive right to employ armed violence. The State is thus equipped, by its very nature, with armed forces. War waged by the State is always just, by definition, since no other authority is entitled to dispute this justice. The State has the sovereign right to decide when recourse to the use of its armed forces is necessary to safeguard its political aims. To question the validity of a war always means questioning the sovereignty and often the stability of the State. This is why, even when it is well-informed, the moral conscience usually remains silent: it does not wish to be accused of jeopardising the survival of the State itself.

Secondly, war is waged by armies. It evolves in line with the development of armaments. Once it is entrusted to armies, war follows its own laws. Outsiders can hardly hope to make their views prevail. The actions of the armed forces are conditioned by the necessity of victory, that is, of the destruction of the enemy's will to oppose the aims determined by the State.

This defines the field of action which is open to the moral conscience. It can intervene in so far as it is allowed either to influence the choice of the aims of the State or else to control the budget of the armed forces. For naturally the activity and the capacity for intervention of the armed forces depend on the military budget. The weaker the armed forces, the less readily will they be called upon to intervene by the State which they serve. The direction of policy depends on the ends which it adopts, but also on the means at its disposal.

But how far may citizens make use in practice of the possibilities of action which are theoretically open to them?

3. THE RIGHTS OF STATES

The State has at its disposal many more means of influencing the conscience of its citizens than the latter have of influencing the conscience of the State. This goes without saying in dictatorships. Yet even in those States with a democratic system which allow their citizens a certain degree of participation, one knows how limited is public participation in the domain of foreign affairs and military matters. The State itself remains in control of most of the information on these questions, and control of information is an almost infallible means of controlling consciences. To obtain exact information concerning foreign relations or military realities is to work for peace, but how difficult this is!

The Americans realised this in the Vietnam situation, but how long this took! As for Central America, how can the truth be discovered? How can one find out the truth about the oil question and the problems of the Middle East? And this is true even in a country where a 'free' press exists!

Furthermore, the State can easily pull the strings of collective emotion. It can stir up for its own purposes deep-rooted feelings which belong to the inmost recesses of national psychology. In the first place, it identifies with the homeland and the people, propagating the belief that the fate and the survival of the people, and the very existence of the country, are bound up with its own fate. In this way, 'patriotism', or traditional attachment to one's native soil, one's culture and one's ancestors, is transferred to the State. Citizens identify with their State as with their homeland. In many parts of the world, this identification is virtually complete. An appeal to patriotism is enough to make citizens close ranks around the State and its flag. In many countries the armed forces are the symbol of the homeland. They are respected and cherished like the homeland itself.

At a level which is perhaps slightly less intense, but which is at times just as strong, the State can play on the religious sentiment of its people. It can persuade them that their religion is in danger if the State does not succeed in enforcing its aims. It mobilises its citizens in the cause of religion. The example of the Moslem States reminds us that this phenomenon is by no means confined to the past. Elsewhere the State may manipulate its people's attachment to their language, their traditions or their culture. It is not easy to demythologise these forms of manipulation. The national principle is very deep-rooted and the peoples of the world are only too inclined to confuse the survival of their country, their religion or their culture with the interests of the State. As, moreover, their attachment to such concepts is an absolute emotion, far stronger than the desire for material possessions or the defence of their social status, it can easily lead to the use of the most radical methods, in other words, military ones. To inveigle a nation into war there is no more effective method than making it believe that its territory, its religion or its language is in danger.

Working for peace involves keeping subjects like the homeland, religion, language or culture as far away as possible from politics. These are explosive matters which can quickly inflame the masses and launch them almost unconsciously on the road to war.

It is indeed true that up to a certain point the State can be a useful or necessary mediator in the conservation of these fundamental areas of national life. But for this very reason the State insists on absolute loyalty from its citizens. It is not, in fact, possible to proclaim one's loyalty to the State in all matters excluding war. Within the present world order and under the impulsion of the principle of national sovereignty, war may be an indispensable instrument of policy. What must then be judged is the policy itself and the limits of a citizen's loyalty to the State in general.

It is vain to urge that the State should have recourse to war in cases only where it is legitimately defending its right. By definition, war is always waged in pursuit of the defence of the rights of the State. It is not an irrational act of violence. The question is far rather what are the rights which the State has the right to defend by war?

At this point it is clearly impossible to define abstract rules. In the final analysis, it is the State which claims the right to define for itself the boundary between those rights which deserve to be defended by war and those which do not.

Some would invoke the right of survival, and yet the survival of a State is rarely called into question. Moreover, there are States which accept a merger with others without feeling offended, for instance the recent case of The Gambia.

There are States which invoke their right to take up arms to defend the integrity of their national territory. This concept of national territory is very vague. The territory controlled by particular States is, in every case, the result of historical accident. Yet this territory often attains a sacred status, in such a way that the loss of an area of territory is the moral equivalent of national ruin and constitutes grounds for war. This is so in most of the border disputes in Latin America. It is so for Argentina or for Great Britain in the case of the Falklands. Certain States cede part of their territory, with or without compensation. Others refuse. Their unwillingness to give up territory increases with their belief that they have sufficient military strength to defend their own point of view.

Certain States consider as grounds for war the defence of a social or economic system, or even the maintenance of a particular form of government. For many, defence against communism and the possibility of the imposition of a communist regime is sufficient to legitimise war. For the communist States themselves the danger of a return to a capitalist system is an obvious *casus belli*. Europe must ask itself the question: Is the defence of the democratic system worth going to war? Is the avoidance of a form of 'Finlandisation' worth a war? What is worth defending by war? Is the economic prosperity of the West something which it is worth fighting to defend?

Some States consider that their security is at stake as soon as certain political or economic advantages are lost. Since 1947 the USA has considered that its national security necessitates the containment of communist expansion within the frontiers between the two world empires drawn by the Yalta agreement. Every communist sortie beyond these limits constitutes grounds for war. This has led to the Korean and Vietnam Wars and a series of open or covert armed interventions in various places in every continent. Naturally, a less powerful State could not entertain such pretensions.

Lastly, certain States feel obliged to go to war by virtue of alliances, mutual defence treaties or implicit solidarity with another State. The credibility of their word is a justification for war. It goes without saying that each State decides on the cases in which it considers itself to be bound by a treaty.

The definition of all these rights, which vary so much with different nations and periods of history, is the responsibility of the State itself. But the State lives in a symbiotic relationship with the population it controls. It can be influenced by its people. Nowadays, more and more, the State takes the form of an immense bureaucracy, extremely inert and extremely unresponsive to explicit influences. Currents of opinion pass through it which are difficult to identify and even more difficult to control. However, at least in those countries where there exists some measure of freedom of opinion and certain organs of communication between the State and its citizens, the latter can intervene to influence the definition of the rights of the State. Generally speaking, the poor and barely educated masses have hardly any chance either of obtaining precise information or of expressing their own opinion. Their voice is channelled through parties or movements, where they exist, which are always, nowadays, very closely linked to the State. Normally, trade unions and other popular organisations are hardly any less bellicose than governments. They are sometimes more so, notably in the United States. In addition, there are social groups or classes which can exert some influence, in particular the major economic groups. Ever increasing heed must be given to the opinion of the armed forces themselves, which are becoming less and less 'silent services'. At the present time they constitute the most important of the State bureaucracies. Often they are a veritable State within the State and their opinion is one of the most important elements which the State must take into account. Obviously this is all the more true of the military States which are so numerous today. Yet even where a civilian State still exists, military influence is important. Here again, the case of the USA is an obvious example.

Can Christians and their churches succeed in forming significant pressure groups?

During the war in Algeria, the Church does not seem to have played an important part in the final French withdrawal. Similarly, where the wars of liberation in the former Portuguese empire were concerned, the Church played an insignificant part: on the contrary, it encouraged the colonial wars of the Salazar regime. On the other hand, churches in the United States seem to have had some degree of influence in ending the Vietnam War, and even more in the withdrawal of US support for the Somoza regime in Nicaragua. As for America's support for the army in El Salvador, the churches are opposing it quite firmly and play an important part amongst the forces opposed to it. At the time of writing (June 1982) they do not appear to have succeeded in changing the strategy of the American government, or its conception of its responsibilities.

In formerly Christian countries, like those of Europe or America, the churches are generally very closely linked to the State by historical, social or institutional ties. It is difficult for them to voice opinions which differ from those of the State. History confirms this: the churches have almost always legitimised wars waged by the State. For example, the churches have legitimised the Falklands War in both Great Britain and Argentina. Moreover, they have their military chaplains who take it upon themselves to proclaim loudly and meaningfully the identity of conscience which exists between Church and State. Confronted by this strong affirmation the timid criticisms which are sometimes uttered by certain churchmen or groups which have no representative status are ineffectual. The churches are against war in general, but in favour of wars in particular cases.

In the new countries of Asia or Africa the churches' position is so weak that they dare not raise their voices. Moreover, the State control of public opinion is such that speaking out would achieve nothing, since news of their action would not even reach the people.

It is self-evident that in every war the two parties are defending real rights which they both consider to justify war. Every international situation is the product of a history which is so complex that every nation can find some grievance against every other nation. Each State always has at its disposal a sufficient number of historical reasons to make war on any other nation. If it does not do so, it is because it is not strong enough or considers that it can obtain sufficient redress for its claim by other means. It is also true that conflicts or rights can lie dormant over a long period. One day they rise to the surface for reasons which are infinitely varied.

Thus, every nation always defends its rights. Of the rights which are in dispute between two States, which are the stronger and can justify the attitude of one of the parties? Generally, it is impossible to give an objective reply to such a question. Usually, the most powerful States are also the most insistent on defending their rights. They find grounds for war in situations in which weaker States would find adequate reasons for negotiation and compromise.

In view of the lack of objective criteria concerning rights, States frequently invoke their national honour. The State is seen as unable to tolerate certain humiliations. In fact it is easy to make its citizens share in the feeling of dishonour and the desire to avenge their country's humiliated honour.

And yet, the criterion of honour is even more arbitrary. The most powerful nations are the most susceptible. The others must practise resignation and transfer their honour elsewhere. For honour can be sublimated. Various peoples can sublimate it through sport, art or archaeology, or even through fashion or the beauty of their women.

4. WHAT ACTION SHOULD BE TAKEN?

A retrospective view of history leads to the conclusion that almost all wars might have been avoided. Conflicts could have been prevented, limited in time, or resolved by other means if an effort had been made quickly enough. The fact is that wars obey autonomous political forces. When timely solutions are not found, politics turns imperceptibly towards war, and after a certain point this process is irreversible.

To avoid war, therefore, there is almost always a political action which is theoretically possible. There are thus, at the origin of war, political errors, weaknesses, some lack of vigilance or insight.

However, politics cannot resolve everything. Mistakes may always happen. It is possible to act on the contexts which encourage recourse to war as a means of self-defence. There are indirect ways of acting upon the State: the dissemination of information, the clarification of political aims and of the rights of the State, the boundaries of national honour, the military budget. The other context consists of the citizens, for peoples are generally as belligerent as, or more belligerent than, their governments. Certain popular emotions are highly dangerous: patriotism, religious feeling, attachment to one's language. These are causes which can easily lead to violence.

As far as Christians and their churches are concerned, they are especially sensitive to religious emotion. In history, there are few motives for war which have shown themselves to be more effective. Religion speedily arouses violence when it feels itself threatened. Thirteen centuries of wars with Islam, centuries of religious wars between Christians, two-thirds of a century of hostility towards communism should warn us. Even today religion is still the best reason for making war. In so far as the churches can control religious emotion, their responsibility is clearly involved.

Translated by L. H. Ginn

Notes

1. See the works quoted and analysed by R. Aron *Penser la guerre, Clausewitz*, II. *L'âge planétaire* (Paris 1976) pp. 268-274.

2. For a brief treatment of this point see our work *La Pouvoir militaire en Amérique latine. L'idéologie de la Sécurité Nationale* (Paris 1977).

3. See R. Aron's discussion of the major contemporary theories in relation to Clausewitz in *Penser la guerre, Clausewitz* (cited in note 1, 2 volumes).

4. See R. Aron *Paix et guerre entre les nations* (Paris 1962).

Mary Evelyn Jegen

An Entirely New Attitude

THE CAREER of Mohandas Gandhi (1869-1948) signals an historic change in the human experience of war as a means of conflict resolution between and among States. Under Gandhi's influence a nation freed itself with non-violent means from the colonial domination of the British Empire. The political event in itself is of major importance because it discredited the myth that revolution and war are inextricably mixed. Perhaps more important was Gandhi's development of a theory and method of non-violent social change, which he labelled *satyagraha* (firm holding to truth). He refined both the theory and method through years of campaigns and accompanying reflection and writing until he was able to say with confidence that *satyagraha* was a science. There remains a fertile field for research into the implications of Gandhi's ideas and methods, and their relationships to other disciplines, as well as to the history of war as experienced in Western culture.

In our long history of war and peace there are four culture strands which have come together to form our present synthesis. From the *Romans* we get our prevailing notions of war as 'diplomacy by other means', our political power exercised by the military, and conversely, of peace as the cessation of armed hostilities and as the condition which follows a war, or which prevails when war is not going on. Both war and peace are perceived as normal, and even inevitable in a cyclic rhythm.

From the *Greeks* we get our notion of peace as harmony, balance, and of war as conflict-writ-large, as disruption of what ought to be.

From our *barbarian ancestors*, or more precisely, from our myths about them, we derive our notions of war as savage and as characteristic of a stage of human development to be transcended by civilisation.

Finally, from our *Judaeo-Christian heritage* we have the concept of peace as *shalom*, integrity of body, mind, spirit, fullness of life and well-being, the richest of blessings. 'Peace I bequeath to you, my own peace I give you, a peace the world cannot give, this is my gift to you' (John 14:27). Notions of war from this tradition are complex and not easily harmonised. The concept of holy war from the Old Testament has had a tremendous influence on our culture. From the New Testament we have derived ideas of a spiritual warfare against the powers of evil; for example, in Ephesians, chapter 6, and also ideas of non-retaliation and love of enemies (Matt. 5 and Luke 6).

1. THE ROAD TO CHANGE

Our modern notions of war are today situated in a new context of interdependence, advanced technology, both an increase in and breakdown of urbanisation, and limits on the way we have been exploiting both non-renewable and renewable resources. It is in this situation that we are experiencing a transformation in the anthropological significance of war. War, which until recently was accepted as a tragic but necessary part of the human condition, is coming to be perceived as itself the arch-enemy of humankind. We are coming to recognise as the most relevant question, not 'Under what conditions should we go to war?' but rather, 'Should we tolerate war at all?'.

(a) Political factors

In the post-colonial age we have come to see more clearly the close connection between injustice and violence, and between peace, liberation, and development, particularly in the conditions which prevail between the industrialised States and their former colonies. After the close of the Second World War these newly independent States found themselves locked into a downward spiral of poverty, oppression, and degradation. The ravages of economic war, though it is not called war, have provoked new kinds of guerilla war and terrorism.

It is in this situation that both an important new concept related to war and a new method of analysing it have emerged. Both are well exemplified in the Palme Report issued in June 1982.[1] The report was drawn up by an independent commission on disarmament and security issues. The seventeen members of the commission were eminent citizens of as many countries, including representatives from Europe, Asia, Africa and America. The underlying premiss of the commission's recommendations is contained in the title of the report: *Common Security: A Programme for Disarmament*. The report recognises that in a world of increasingly interdependent economies, security can be provided only if nations begin to organise their security policies in co-operation with one another. The adage, 'Peace through strength', to the extent that it is meant to convey the impression that strength is measured by military superiority, is no longer useful.

Another major factor in the transformation of the meaning of war has been the set of assumptions propelling the development of new military technology. We do well to remember that the climate in which atomic weapons were used in 1945 was one which tolerated or espoused such values as absolute national sovereignty, the nation at arms, total victory, and unconditional surrender, and which had already seen saturation bombing and other acts of war clearly outside the bounds of acceptable moral behaviour. On the one hand, the use of atomic weaponry was a logical expression of 'total war'; on the other hand, its use began an upward spiral in a politics of mutual threat which now expresses itself in an arms race accurately described in a statement from the Vatican as a machine gone mad.

There is no coherent theoretical structure underlying the arms race. It is generally perceived as an unfortunate necessity, an expression of a policy of deterrence. Deterrence is a notion which contains inner contradictions. The goal of deterrence is to defend and to provide security through the prevention of the use of nuclear weapons in war. The means to this goal, in deterrence policy, is to threaten the perceived enemy with retaliation of such massive proportions that it would make a nuclear attack useless, and therefore unreasonable. In this posture of mutual threat of massive retaliation, the antagonists call on each other to negotiate arms control. They also develop a public posture favouring eventual disarmament.

Though there is a growing understanding of the danger of the doctrine of deterrence, and also of its inner contradictions, widespread acceptance of deterrence as a necessity has made possible the tolerance and support of an ever-increasing race for superiority, as an insurance against possible inferiority in perceived military strength, even while lip

service is paid to the quest for equivalence or parity between the two major antagonists
in the arms race, the United States and the Soviet Union. Even while the two major
antagonists are attempting negotiations, each is promoting the development of
'qualitatively superior' (i.e., capable of more rapid and massive death-dealing)
weapons. Thus, there is a resurgence of chemical weapons and the prospect of the
application of laser technology to weaponry to be used in outer space. This behaviour
flows from a recognition that it is impossible to measure equivalence, since kinds and
numbers of weapons must be considered in a broad geopolitical context in order to come
to some understanding of their effectiveness in use. A submarine carrying missiles with
multiple warheads cannot be accurately measured against a land-based missile. Soviet
tanks situated on the Eurasian land mass are not equivalent to the same kinds of tanks in
the United States.

What maintains deterrence as a political belief is fear of the unprecedented danger
inherent in military technology which is now capable of destroying civilisation itself. In
1975, Pope Paul VI called the atomic bombing of Hiroshima a *'butchery of untold
magnitude'*. The potential for repeating and magnifying that butchery has now increased
so far that it is beyond imagination.

There is clearly no way to unlearn military technology. Hope is grounded rather in
the possibility of constructing a new politics which rejects war and replaces it with a way
of *conflict resolution* not dependent on legalised killing as a means. This is the historic
struggle of our time.

The possibility of such a transformation to a new way of thinking depends on a
broad-based supportive climate of opinion now developing. Evidence includes the
proliferation of books, articles, and media presentations on nuclear weapons issues, the
dramatic mass demonstrations in European cities in the fall of 1981 and in the United
States in June 1982, special sessions on disarmament in the United Nations in 1978 and
1982, a remarkable swelling of the numbers of conscientious objectors, the organised
international efforts of physicians against the threat of nuclear war, the campaign of the
Interchurch Peace Council in the Netherlands, with its powerful slogan, 'Help Rid the
World of Nuclear Weapons. Let it Begin in the Netherlands', the international
movement begun in the United States calling for a bilateral halt to any further
production of nuclear weapons, and many more. Disarmament is now widely perceived
as the most urgent public issue of our time. All are involved because all are vulnerable.

(b) Catholic Social Teaching on Peace and War

In the social teaching of the Church on issues related to nuclear weapons and nuclear
war there is not yet a clearly definable line of developing teaching. *A theology of peace*
has become an urgent pastoral need, and within the body of pronouncements on peace,
war, and related issues there are certainly elements for such a theology. However, there
is lacking an adequate framework for treating some of the most pressing questions
relating to nuclear deterrence and to the possession and manufacture of nuclear
weapons.

Two related streams of the Church's teaching need to be distinguished: one, a
positive teaching about peace, and the other, a teaching about a Christian response to
violence, especially the armed violence of war. Besides this division, there is another
distinction, equally important but more problematic. On the one hand, some Catholic
theologians and ethicists approach issues of war relying heavily on the just war tradition
of the Stoics, first brought into the Church by St Augustine. This tradition provides both
a framework and an analytical tool for arguing the morality of policies and actions. On
the other hand, especially since the Second Vatican Council, more and more
theologians are calling for a framework that is more openly biblical in its grounding,

relying especially on the teaching of Jesus about unconditional love and forgiveness of enemies.

It confuses the issue badly to label this second approach 'pacifist', since 'pacifist', as generally used, means the unwillingness to use armed force, and little or nothing more. Gospel non-violence, as it is being studied and communicated in today's context, includes a repudiation of legalised armed violence, but it does not mean passivity. Gospel non-violence calls for the *active intervention* of love in conflict situations. It calls for *constructive works of justice* and peacemaking, not for *withdrawal from struggle*.

The Church's modern constructive teaching on peace is most strongly expressed in the encyclical *Pacem in Terris* (1963) in which Pope John XXIII sets the problems related to war within the context of human rights. Within this framework, *Pacem in Terris* clearly demonstrates a crying need for a transnational juridical order corresponding to an emerging transnational moral order based on ever-growing human interdependence. The alternative to the construction of such an international order will be the disintegration of such elements of a common good as have already been achieved. The arms race is seen as a consequence of the failure to express and foster the common good.

The encyclical notes the argument that the production of arms can be justified on the grounds that in present-day conditions peace cannot be preserved without an equal balance of armaments, but it goes on to argue that this is an error based on a false understanding of humankind and society. John is quite clear that disarmament is dependent on sincere co-operation 'to banish the fear and anxious expectation of war with which people are oppressed' (art. 113).

Here peace is regarded as a *human construction* that depends fundamentally not on a response to individual conflicts between nations but on a *vision of humankind* which affirms the ability, and more than an ability, a human right, that is, an inherent claim to live in truth, justice, love, and freedom. Mutual trust is a condition for the exercise of these powers, hence all that can foster trust is the work of peace.

Two years later, *Gaudium et Spes* made a signal advance in the constructive teaching on peace by a clear affirmation of non-violence: 'We cannot fail to praise those who renounce the use of violence in the vindication of their rights and who resort to methods of defence which are otherwise available to weaker parties too, provided that this can be done without injury to the rights and duties of others or of the community itself' (art. 78). Some would see that the qualifying clause at the end of this sentence weakens the statement. However, read in context, there is a strong affirmation for a way of peacemaking not dependent on military strength, a way, or ways, which can be engaged in without neglecting one's responsibilities towards others' rights. There is an acknowledgment that the threat of war will hang over us until the return of Christ, but a refusal to accept war itself fatalistically, for 'to the extent that people vanquish sin by a union of love, they will vanquish violence as well and make these words come true: "They shall beat their swords into ploughshares and their spears into pruning hooks; one nation shall not raise the sword against another, nor shall they train for war again" ' (Isa. 2:4). The main thrust of the Church's teaching on war since Pope John XXIII is not an application of the Roman view of peace as the consequence of terminating a war, but of peace in the Judaeo-Christian view, as *shalom*, fullness of life, as both blessing and human achievement. Peace is seen as an enterprise of justice, as the fruit of love, and Christians are 'to join with all true peacemakers in pleading for peace and bringing it about' (GS, art. 78).

The relationship between justice and peace is developed more fully in the encyclical *Populorum Progressio*, which calls integral human development including its social, economic and political dimensions 'the new name for peace'. The institution of the Pontifical Commission Justice and Peace within the Roman Curia in 1967 is an institutional expression of this constructive. Peace teaching, which has been continued strongly by Pope John Paul II in many ways, notably in his World Day of Peace messages, beginning with 'To Reach Peace, Teach Peace' (1979), continued in the encyclical *Redemptor Hominis*, and in many of his addresses during his visits to various countries. Characteristic of John Paul's teaching on peace is his absolute refusal to settle for any attitudes of determinism or anxious resignation to war as a necessary part of the human condition. Thus, in 'To Reach Peace, Teach Peace', he describes as universal principles: 'Recourse to arms cannot be considered the right means for settling conflicts', and 'It is not permissible to kill in order to impose a solution.' In 1981, in Hiroshima, he spoke of war as a human practice which must be abandoned.

In the face of the man-made calamity that every war is, one must affirm and reaffirm, again and again, that the waging of war is not inevitable or unchangeable. Humanity is not destined to self-destruction.

Clashes of ideologies, aspirations and needs can and must be settled and resolved by means other than war and violence. Humanity owes it to itself to settle differences and conflicts by peaceful means.

A year later, speaking in Coventry, England, he repeated the position, saying: 'Today the scale and the horror of modern warfare—whether nuclear or not—makes it totally unacceptable as a means of settling differences between nations.' There could hardly be a clearer indication of an approach to peace and war that does not lean on the just war tradition.

This is not surprising, since there is no mention of the just war tradition in *Gaudium et Spes*. The argument from silence is a powerful one when the question is raised about the continuing usefulness or appropriateness of the tradition for dealing with contemporary problems of war and peace. *Gaudium et Spes*, after a review of the '*horror and perversity of war* . . . immensely magnified by the multiplication of scientific weapons' declares that 'all these considerations compel us to undertake an evaluation of war with an entirely new attitude' (art. 80).

It is this new attitude which is so remarkably demonstrated by Pope John Paul II. He spoke in Hiroshima about the future of life on this planet as dependent 'upon one single factor: *Humanity must make a moral about-face*'. He continued:

The task is enormous; some will call it a Utopian one. But how can we fail to sustain the trust of modern man against all the temptations to fatalism, to paralysing passivity, to moral dejection? We must say to the people of today: Do not doubt, your future is in your own hands. The building of a more just humanity or a more united international community is not just a dream or a vain ideal. It is a moral imperative, a sacred duty, one that the intellectual and spiritual genius of humankind can face, through a fresh mobilisation of everybody's talents and energies, through putting to work all the technical and cultural resources of the human family.

It is the context of this unmistakable thrust of the Church's teaching on the real possibility of peace as fruit of a human vocation to love and justice that we should assess the passages in the documents which speak specifically to such matters as the arms race, disarmament, and the use of nuclear weapons as a deterrent. In the only condemnation by the Council, *Gaudium et Spes* declares that 'Any act of war aimed indiscriminately at the destruction of entire cities or of extensive areas along with their population is a crime against humankind itself. It merits unequivocal and unhesitating condemnation' (art. 80).

Gaudium et Spes is not so forthright when speaking of deterrence. Recognising deterrence as a 'capacity for immediate retaliation against an adversary', the passage notes that 'many regard this state of affairs as the most effective way by which peace of a sort can be maintained between nations at the present time' (art. 81). But *Gaudium et Spes* does not approve deterrence. Rather, it declares:

> Whatever be the case with this method of deterrence, men should be convinced that the arms race in which so many countries are engaged is not a safe way to preserve a steady peace. Nor is the so-called balance resulting from this race a sure and authentic peace. Rather than being eliminated thereby, the causes of war threaten to grow gradually stronger. (*Ibid.*)

Since the Council there has been a noticeable shift in the language used to describe the arms race. *Gaudium et Spes* calls it 'an utterly treacherous trap for humanity, and one which injures the poor to an intolerable degree' (*Ibid.*). In 1974 it is described as 'an insanity' and in 1976 as 'a machine gone mad'.[2] The language signals a shift in perception, from seeing the arms race as a problem which can be brought under control by reason, to a view of the arms race as a problem calling for more than a political solution. It is rather a pervasive disorder that requires a cure at a deeper, cultural level.

Several conferences of bishops have clarified and pushed the teaching of *Pacem in Terris* and *Gaudium et Spes* to its logical consequences. The Medellín Conference of Latin American Bishops (1968) developed the constructive elements of a peace theology, and in so doing gave a good example of an emerging method for properly locating specific problems of violence. Three dimensions of peace provide the framework in which the Latin American bishops address the problem of violence in Latin America: peace as the work of justice, peace as permanent task, peace as the fruit of love. The bishops speak forcefully to the situation of the institutionalised violence of political and economic exploitation, and also to the question of armed violence in liberation efforts. While showing deep sympathy for those victimised by institutional violence who look to armed revolt as a justifiable last resort, they come down clearly favourable to strategies of non-violence.

The National Conference of Catholic Bishops of the United States has extended and applied the teaching of *Gaudium et Spes* on the question of nuclear weapons, in the pastoral letter, *To Live in Christ Jesus* (1976). The pastoral treats the issue in the context of American society, and states: 'As possessors of a vast nuclear arsenal, we must also be aware that not only is it wrong to attack civilian populations but it is also wrong to threaten to attack them as part of a strategy of deterrence.'

(c) Implications of Christian Participation in the Peace Movement

Christians, both in Europe and in the United States, are in many instances leading the popular peace movement, and if we include, as we should, the struggle for justice in Latin America as part of the larger peace movement, Christians are the architects of the peace movement there also. The cutting edge of the Christian participation is in the form of resistance to current policies: in Europe, to rid Europe of nuclear weapons; in the United States, to resist the arms build-up and to call on the United States and the Soviet Union to declare a halt to any further manufacture of nuclear weapons; in countries in Central and South America, to overcome what the bishops at Medellín correctly label structural violence which destroys the poor and provokes among the oppressed recourse to violent revolution as a last resort.

Increasingly there is a resort to more than verbal opposition, though there will continue to exist a need for clear teaching on the meaning of peace, and a critique of government policies. Protest now takes the form of increasing numbers of Christians declaring themselves conscientious objectors to military service on the grounds that they cannot follow orders to use nuclear weapons or to collaborate in any way with a military which is committed to serve the declared policy of willingness to use strategic nuclear weapons. Christians are also increasingly expressing through tax resistance their opposition to war preparation. In the United States one archbishop has declared publicly that he is withholding 50 per cent of his income taxes as a protest against the nuclear arms race.

Another arena for the peace movement is the work place, with some Christians giving up employment in weapons manufacture as a matter of conscience, and many others gathering to pray and demonstrate at weapons manufacturing plants. In the United States a diocese has established a solidarity fund to help workers who give up employment in a local nuclear weapons plant.

Civil disobedience also takes the form of deliberately damaging nuclear weapons components. The controversy aroused by these actions serves to establish a teaching and learning environment for issues of peace and war. To educate public opinion is one of the direct goals, and possibly the most direct goal of at least some of those who engage in civil disobedience. The increase of such actions is a powerful stimulus to more critical thinking.

There is a growing ecumenical dimension to the Christian peace movement. In the Netherlands the Interchurch Peace Council has been a most important change agent in the peace movement there, and has also been influential in stimulating movements in other countries and in America. A group of Protestants and Catholics from the United States has asked to spend Peace Week in the Netherlands to study the methodology of Peace Week and of other activities of the Council, including its political strategies, in order to see how they may be adapted to the peace movement in the churches in the United States.

An ecumenical New Abolitionist Covenant movement originating in the United States is also influencing the European peace movement in Europe. The New Abolitionist Covenant originated in a series of retreats made by a small group of members of five religious peace groups, including the Fellowship of Reconciliation, Pax Christi, New Call to Peacemaking (a programme of the historic peace churches in the United States), Sojourners, and the Church of the Saviour, the last two with large evangelical Protestant memberships. In less that a year more than 500,000 copies of the covenant texts were distributed. It is estimated that more than a million persons have made a covenant to work to abolish nuclear weapons, and to do this in response to their faith. The social efficacy of the New Abolitionist Covenant springs in part from its drawing on the early abolitionist movement in the United States which brought an end to slavery after more than 200 years of social acceptance. In the nuclear weapons abolitionist movement there is a powerful use of symbols and a drawing on memories of faith and patriotism.

2. ROOTS OF THE TRANSFORMATION

Having reviewed changes in attitudes towards war and peace as expressed in both the larger society and in the Church, it is now possible to make some generalisations and to attempt an analysis.

First, there is clearly a struggle to repudiate the belief that war is inevitable. This intellectual struggle has been provoked in large part by the sheer magnitude and horror of modern weaponry and the danger it poses to the very survival of civilisation and the planet itself. How one experiences the prospect of war in the future depends almost

E

entirely on how one experiences human freedom, and even more basically, how one experiences reality. For those who tend, consciously or not, towards extreme philosophical realism, war will be seen as inevitable, or nearly so. Those who tend to extreme idealism will see war as 'obsolete'. The critical realist will see war as something that must be made obsolete by human action, and that can be outlawed, though this will not happen inevitably, and not without an extraordinary intellectual and moral conversion.

While it may be fear and a shudder of horror which has been the catalyst for a shift in attitudes and perception about war, there is also a growing recognition of the fact and possibilities of non-violent conflict resolution which spurs people on to protest the arms race and to come up with more creative approaches to conflict resolution. Drawing on the experience of non-violent conflict resolution on the interpersonal level, in marriage, family, and community life, and also in labour-management disputes and other professional situations, people nourish fresh hope that there exists the human capability to apply non-violent methods of conflict resolution to conflicts between and among States. It is in this connection that the career of Gandhi is so significant.

Coupled with this is the growing recognition that the purpose for which wars were fought cannot be achieved by a widespread war using 'qualitatively superior' (i.e., more lethal) weapons, and that the risk of waging nuclear war outweighs the risks of repudiating it as a matter of policy. In short, war is seen as irrational, and therefore evokes rejection.

The new attitude towards war is also coloured by a greater understanding of the links between war and injustice. The crassness and venality of the international arms trade is receiving both greater exposure and greater resistance. There is also a growing body of evidence supporting the claim that the arms race is a factor in declining domestic economies, reflected in growing unemployment and the elimination of basic social services.

On the other hand, there are pressures retarding the shift to an entirely new attitude towards war. The greatest of these pressures springs from a more pervasive and subtle greed than that expressed by a small number of arms profiteers. It is becoming ever more clear that an unjust international economic order supports an arms race in its own defence. The other side of this is that we cannot be serious about peacemaking without facing the cost in terms of relinquishing economic power over other peoples and nations. We must transform the *power of domination* into *collaborative power* expressed in new kinds of economic, social, and political arrangements. In this regard, the North-South axis, separating the affluent minority from an economically depressed and oppressed majority of the world's people, is as important, if not more important, than the East-West axis which divides nations ideologically.

As the struggle for a constructive peacemaking continues, we can expect to see it united with the *human rights movement*. Just as the world food crisis, which was perceived precisely as a crisis early in 1970, gave rise to the notion of a right to food, so the nuclear threat may give rise to human rights terminology related to peace. We will, for example, possibly hear less of conscientious objection, and more of the affirmation of the right to refuse to kill. This right will be exercised by others besides those liable to military conscription. It will also be claimed by those forced by economic circumstances to manufacture weaponry, and by citizens who claim the right to refuse to finance military operations through taxes.

The opening words of *Gaudium et Spes* remind us that the joys, hopes, griefs, and anxieties of all people are the joys, hopes, griefs, and anxieties of the followers of Christ who participate in the same history. Since those words were written, anxiety has become a hallmark of our time, an anxiety provoked by the *wedding of technology with an outmoded belief in war as somehow inevitable. Gaudium et Spes* also reminds us that we need to evaluate war with an entirely new attitude and calls attention to the growing conviction that war can no longer be viewed as an apt means for settling disputes, no matter how grievous.

3. REDEMPTIVE BREAKTHROUGH

In what is happening today we can see the human imagination struggling to bring itself into line with the implications of weapons technology and the military and political beliefs which undergird it. The first thirty-six years of attempting to come to terms with nuclear militarism have brought us to a new stage of crisis. We may now be at the *edge of a redeeming breakthrough*.

There is clearly a need for a new frame of reference in which to handle the perennial problems of international conflict. Conflict arises from opposing claims to the same goods or territory, or from the threat of loss of an entire way of life. The new situation of militarism which promises losses greater than any possible gains has provoked us to probe more deeply the depths of human experience, and to ask more honestly about the relationship of war and peace. Widespread fear and anxiety bring home to us our fundamental fear of death. Ultimately the cure for that fear is not a personal effort to save life at any cost, or a social and political effort to defend it by conquering our enemies. On both the personal and social levels, the cure is in the risk to love.

The acceptance of the just war tradition for over 1500 years has legitimised the socially organised killing of war, and has eroded our sense of the political dimension of love. The religious legitimation of killing has also prevented our culture from coming to a mature response to the fear of death, and to the insight that it is better to bear evil than to inflict it, and better still to change conflicts from situations of power as dominance to power as relational in some framework of mutuality. This is what Gandhi meant when he explained that *satyagraha* changes a situation from one in which one sides loses and the other wins, to a situation in which both parties win.

While the just war theory may have been useful to moralists, it has not been functional for generals and their subordinates. Today, under the conditions of nuclear weapons technology, we are all threatened by the legalised killing of war. This has provoked a fresh scrutiny of the just war tradition. It has sent us back to the roots of the Christian ethic, grounded in a biblical theology. We are only at the first stages of developing a geniune biblical theology of peace. What is emerging is a fresh look at the unconditional character of Christian love, validated especially in love of enemies. This is the 'new commandment' of Jesus which history has now made an imperative.

This biblical insight corresponds to the political insight that security cannot be provided within a framework of absolute national sovereignties competing with each other, but that we can have security only if we aim for it as a common security. This, in turn, helps make clear that we need to replace *owning* with *sharing* as the goal for the management of the world's resources. Consciously aiming for sharing the earth's resources according to an established ranking or prioritising of human needs could provide a constructive framework for arms negotiations, since gradual steps towards reductions could be linked to offers to allocate access to needed resources.

An ethic guided by the value of sharing as having priority over the value of owning would be informed, for Christians, by a vision of the fundamental unity of the human family as imaged by Jesus and developed theologically in the New Testament.

A final observation: The elements of a constructive peace theology seem to be emerging more quickly and strongly in practice than in theological literature. This is a sign of authenticity, and it can lead us to expect a coming theological dialogue marked by a great vigour.

Notes

1. *Common Security: A Programme for Disarmament.* Issued under the chairmanship of Olaf Palme (London 1982) pp. 202.

2. The arms race is called an 'insanity' in a statement issued during the 1974 Roman Synod; it is called a 'machine gone mad' in a document presented by the Holy See to a United Nations special committee for the study of disarmament (1976).

Adolfo Pérez Esquivel

Listening to the Silence of God

CONCILIUM HAS asked me for this contribution on justice and peace, some reflections on my experiences in accompanying and sharing the journey of the people of God, in Latin America, a continent living between anguish and hope.

All roads lead somewhere, they cross, disappear over sometimes unknown horizons, and they serve to interweave cultures and languages. They thus superimpose and gather in the signs of the times, the history of the peoples, that history which is rarely told. Roads which are not travelled generate neither past nor present history, they die in oblivion.

Known history is not always true history, but that taught by the rulers. In Latin America we are taught this badly-told history. This history of our conquerors, which fashioned the prototype of the warrior heroes and forgot or did not want us to know the history lived by the peoples, our indigenous peoples, their spirit, their language, their culture, their martyrs, their longings for freedom and justice, their distress, their sufferings, their constantly repaired roads of hope. History transmitted from mouth to mouth, from hand to hand, with prospects of new dawns.

To live in Latin America is to share this rich mosaic of different indigenous cultures, of conquered conquistadors, of Black peoples inserted against their will in the continent and who, by dint of suffering and need, made it theirs by their own will; of peasants, workers, young people, religious, establishing themselves on the land; of the Church with its burden of conquests, sharing the power of the rulers, and this newly emergent face of the Church, invading, penetrating, evangelising, liberating. For all these reasons, it is impossible to speak of a uniform, abstract Latin America. It does have common roots and needs, a force of unity not fully understood but intensely lived. And it is with this people, with their spirituality, their contradictions, poverties and hopes that today, at the crossroads, we can see and feel where we as Christians understand our obligations.

In the complex world we live in, in which the great scientific and technical advances, space travel, cybernetics, are interwoven with hunger, war, the oppression of peoples; in this world, the ambitions of power, dependence, marginalisation and exploitation are structures of injustice which grow when man is forgotten. And when man forgets man he also forgets God and loses all his *raison d'être*, becomes an object and not a subject, our brother and son of God. This even occurs among so-called Christians.

The little brother Charles de Foucauld bore witness to these profound concerns of 'shouting the Gospel with one's whole life', of imitating and sharing the life of the poor, like Jesus, to the point of dying for those he loved.

And it is with this total availability that, even in the tumult of our great cities, we must create an inner wilderness, a wilderness that allows us to listen to the silence of God, our Lord of history, who in the signs of the times implores and points the way to each of us. To listen to the silence of God is the prayer of living, sharing and understanding this untold history of the poor, the humble and the oppressed of the people of God, to contribute to the construction of his kingdom and his justice. And it is from these roads covered over long years of travelling and sharing the life of the peoples of Latin America that I want to indicate some signs that have penetrated me, helped by the wisdom of the simple. Wisdom is a gift granted to the simple in heart. It is born of the reflection on the Faith, of the grass-roots Church communities. It is hope and power of the Spirit. These signs I wish to share as a little brother who for a long time has resisted putting into writing these experiences, very often lived with pain, and who knows his limitations in transmitting them fully. These signs are crossroads in the roads shared by the Church in Latin America, and indicate in some way the fears and hopes of the peoples.

1 – Christians faced with war.
  The absurd has become a daily fact. The Falklands war—April 1982.
2 – A new face for the Church, poor, prophetic, bearing witness. End of the Constantinian epoch in the Latin American Church—Meeting of the Latin American bishops in the Hogar de la Santa Cruz, Riobamba, 12 August 1966.
3 – 'God does not kill'—Experiences of prison—The silence of God. Wilderness and prayer—April 1977.
4 – Wisdom of the humble—Peace and love are the same thing. Signs of hope—Recife, Brazil, May 1981.

1. CHRISTIANS FACED WITH WAR

We are experiencing the consequences of a war: destruction, death, physical, mental and spiritual mutilation.

They went off to war with cries of enthusiasm and victory, almost like a festival. And conquerors and conquered returned defeated, with the bitter taste of destruction. Justifications have been put forward. There has been much discussion on the justice of war. Saint Augustine, Saint Thomas, and many others have pointed out the conditions in articles, but it is necessary for us Christians to make an effort to understand and live more profoundly the message of the Gospel. When Christians believe more in the temporal powers and in the power of weapons than in Gospel, they loss the strength of God.

The Falklands war confronted us with situations difficult to reconcile. Some bishops, priests, religious, Christians in general raised warlike voices, even louder than the military, justifying the war, the destruction of the enemy. To speak of peace was almost equal to treason. They used religion, God, the rosary, the Virgin, as justifications of war.

We also heard signs of hope: some bishops and Christian groups who, with a spirit in harmony with the Gospel, proclaimed peace as a fundamental value of life.

I received a lot of criticisms and insults solely for declaring that no just wars exist, only just causes. All war is unjust. Not believing this, we justify the atrocities which are born of the very concept of war: to destroy the enemy.

These contradictions among Christians, these justifications, have led the world to live in a balance of terror, with the increase in atomic arsenals, with more and more sophisticated weapons and more technological wars, with science at the service of destruction and traders in death.

'During the whole Constantinian epoch', writes Father J. Comblin, 'the theory of the just war served to exonerate the support that the Church ordered its faithful to lend to emperors, kings, States or whatever other power allied to it. Except for exceptional cases the Church did not contest the wars undertaken by kings, but rather justified them.' And drawing on those texts he passed an even more categorical judgment: 'The aim of doctrine is manifestly to give permission to make war' (*Théologie de la Paix*, Ed. Universitaires, Paris, 1963, vol. II, p. 18).

We could continue with a long history of justifications, but it is not my intention to embark on a theological study of the subject, merely to highlight a few points.

John Paul II stated during his visit to Great Britain: 'At this moment mankind should question itself yet again on the absurd and always unjust phenomenon of war.' On his arrival in Argentina he said: 'The sad sight of the losses in human life, with social consequences that will last for quite some time among the peoples who suffer war, make me think with profound distress of the trail of death and desolation that any armed conflict always provokes.' Legitimate defence is invoked, the same means and resorts as the aggressor. Thus from the legitimacy of defence one arrives at the legitimacy of homicidal violence.

Christ gives us a clear and decisive order: 'Do not kill.' This is nothing but an order.

In the Falklands War, absurd like any war, made behind the backs of the people, at a time when the country is undergoing oppression and poverty and a serious spiritual and moral crisis, many voices have been raised in support of it, even from Christian sectors, and they have tried to justify it in every way: 'From an evil like war good things can emerge for the Argentinians . . . Christians cannot fail in support (for the war), on pain of renouncing their double identity—religious and national' (*La Tarde*, Tucumán, 7 June 1982. *Los cristianos y la guerra*, I. López).

In this way political, economic and military interests overcome the Gospel, and the Word of God and commitment are not followed.

I only wish to point out the need for a profound re-examination of the position of Christians with regard to war and its clarification. The popular struggles, the liberation movements, do not necessarily have to be conceived in terms of armed action.

2. A NEW FACE FOR THE CHURCH: POOR, PROPHETIC, BEARING WITNESS

Paul VI recommended to the bishops that they exchange pastoral experiences and meet to share and be in contact. In this fraternal spirit, a group of Latin American bishops periodically holds meetings to this end, mutually assisting one another in reflection and in order to establish closer links in the march of the Latin American and universal Church. This group of bishops has been joined by some priests and laity, to assist strictly pastoral reflection within the Latin American reality and the problems experienced by the Church and the peoples.

The participants come from various countries of the continent (Mexico, Brazil, Chile, Peru, Colombia, Ecuador, Argentina, Venezuela, Paraguay), and also from the United States.

Although at the time the repressive actions of the government of Ecuador against the bishops and participants in the Hogar de la Santa Cruz, Riobamba, the diocese headed by Mgr. Proano, had international repercussions and disturbed the Church, because of what the detention of so many bishops, religious and laity signified, afterwards it was dismissed as just one of those things.

None the less, I believe that this fact marks in the Latin American Church the end of the Constantinian epoch, of alliances between governments and the Church and the sharing of temporal power. 'When Christianity became the religion of the Empire, then the stoic and political virtues of the Empire began to supplant the original theological virtues of the early Christians. The heroism of the soldier supplanted the heroism of the martyr' (Thomas Merton, *Conjectures of a Guilty Bystander*, 1968, p. 87).

To those who experienced those moments of repression it made clearer to us this new, emergent face of the Church which is searching to be more poor, prophetic, witnessing; this move to be people of God: 'You will be persecuted in my name, but fear not. . . .' A completely new phenomenon in our continent where the temporal powers—who declare themselves Christian and fly the flag of so-called Christian and Western civilisation and its defence through the ideology of national security—repress the people and those, as in Riobamba, who take on the task of living the Gospel together with the poor and needy. This event is a sign from God that questions and appeals to us as Christians.

Mgr. Enrique Alvear, Auxiliary Bishop of Santiago, Chile, on his return to Chile, together with the bishops Mgr. González and Mgr. Aristia, stated: 'With a heart full of peace, joy and hope, without any resentment or bitterness towards anyone. On the contrary, knowing that all that is pain, humiliation, always, according to the Gospel, is converted into a source of joy, of salvation, of benefits for mankind.' And he made reference to the action of the Church in the liberation of mankind in Latin America; liberation as understood by the Gospel: complete.

This means that it is a highly positive sign of this Church which is renewing itself and in which the bishops stop being the individual pastor of a diocese isolated from the context of the world, and begin to be the pastor who belongs to a college of bishops responsible for the Church and for evangelising the whole world, at all levels. A commitment which leads the Church to live the martyrdom of many of its sons and is the seed of hope for a more just and human world. The sadness and joy experienced in the Hogar de la Santa Cruz, in this meeting transformed into a sign from God, could be said to have been crystallised in the moment experienced during the celebration of the Eucharist in the district of San Ignacio in Quito, where they were taken off and detained: the mass conducted by Mgr. Enrique Alvear and Mgr. Carlos González was a strongly felt presence ('Where two or three are gathered together in my name, I am among them . . .'). Surrounded by officers and men of the military police, when the greeting of peace came, we also stretched out our hands to them. They looked at us, taken aback. Their plan of intolerance and injustice was disarmed by the force of the spirit of the weak.

This is the path of the Latin American Church, a sign of hope and light for the world.

3. 'GOD DOES NOT KILL'

After Riobamba, Ecuador, we decided to return to Argentina. The grave situation, of terrorism generated by guerrilla warfare and by the repression unleashed by the Armed Forces and Security Forces, continued. There were thousands of dead, abducted; prisons and tortures which affected all sectors of the country: trade union, political, educational, cultural, and even the Church, with priests assassinated and nuns disappearing.

On 4 April I was arrested and taken to the superintendence of Federal Security, and put in a 'tube', a small cell with no light and no sanitary fittings, where I lived for thirty-two days, in which day and night were the same. When I was being led to the 'tube', I was aware in the darkness of a strong smell of urine, sweat and fear. The iron door was locked behind me. At times I heard the sound of gratings and the step of the guard. It was the first day of Holy Week and the anniversary of the death of Martin Luther King.

To accustom myself to it, I had to use touch rather than sight; a thin, damp mattress on the floor, and a space of three paces from the door to the wall. When we are plunged into a place without dimensions, time loses its meaning. We can guess very much. Prayer is hurried over, haphazardly, is broken off unfinished. Slowly I understood that I had to recover my inner calm. When we pray at normal times, we generate certain favourable conditions so that our prayer can fully develop. In extreme situations everything is transformed and we discover a new dimension of the power of prayer, the need to create an inner wilderness and listen to the silence of God within us.

The hours passed. I heard steps and voices. Someone turned the lock and slid back the bolt on the door. When it was opened the light blinded me. I managed to see a lot of graffiti on the walls. Every two days I was allowed to walk for a little in an enclosed rectangular area, where there were also other 'tubes'. The place was a torture centre. During my stay they only took women from other prisons, for transfer or release granted, at night. The majority were from the interior of the country, arrested without trial or reason. One elderly woman whose companions called her 'Grandma' told me: 'Son . . . I have cried so much I have no tears left. I am dried up inside. They have done so much harm I want them to pay for so much injustice. . . .' Fear, faltering words, uncertainty. Also a little gleam of hope for freedom.

Some young people had been abducted who had been in unknown places. There they were 'legalised'. During those days in which I could walk in the enclosure, I began to pay attention to the graffiti in the 'tubes'. I remember some: 'In the evening of life they will call for you in love' . . . 'Father, forgive them, they know not what they do'. . . 'Virgin, save us, we are innocent'. Insults, names of loved ones, of a favourite club; and a large dark mark. Later I discovered it was blood. With this blood three words had been written: 'God does not kill'. I often think of them, as though they were engraved inside me. When the guard locked me in the 'tube', in total darkness, these three words were in me. I reflected a lot on this, on this tortured brother who in a moment of extremity made this profound act of faith and wrote with his own blood 'God does not kill'. It is the heart-rendering cry of a whole people. We must go into these questions deeply. Many atrocities have been perpetrated in the name of Christian and Western civilisation. A dirty war has broken out for which all means are valid. It is the total negation of life and of God.

4. WISDOM OF THE HUMBLE

During an extensive journey around Brazil, together with Dom Helder Cámara, Archbishop of Olinda and Recife, we visited one of the shanty towns of his diocese, on the banks of a river which, when it is in flood, inundates the flimsy housing. The poverty, this structural injustice which overwhelms the poorest peoples, was felt everywhere. Under the burning sun of Recife, we entered the town, accompanied by its inhabitants who were worried by a possible eviction. The majority earn less than the minimum wage and are scarcely able to feed themselves. A lot of children followed us. Among the crowd, a black woman, with a perspiring and worn face, poorly dressed and barefoot, a rag on her head, like the peasant women of the north-east, came up to us smiling, her eyes alive with great happiness. She was carrying two wild flowers gathered on the river bank. She handed me the white flower, saying: 'This white flower is the symbol of peace', and turning to Dom Helder she handed him the red flower: 'This red flower is the symbol of love'. She joined her hands and said to us: 'Peace and love are the same thing.' Then, in silence, she joined the train of people accompanying us. When we reached the centre of the town they explained their situation: the promises from government officials which were never fulfilled; their needs; their histories. The majority were from the interior, workers who had lost their lands through long droughts and bad harvests, or who did not have the means to subsist. They are part of the massive migrations to the urban centres in search of better chances of living and working.

The sun was drying up the earth. The heat had become more intense. Among the people, the woman of the white and red flowers smiled with the wisdom of the simple, full of hope. In spite of her uncertain tomorrow and her deprivations.

A lot of strength is needed, and courage; much faith in God, to live and survive in these conditions, to fight to be a person and not be crushed by injustice.

Justice consists in re-establishing the truth and the right of the individual and of peoples. The right to freedom, to a more just and human life.

Today the Church of Latin America is rediscovering its prophetic mission, its preferential option for the poor, being the Church of the people of God.

These four testimonies, apparently unconnected, are, none the less, closely united in spirit, and they indicate at the same time the contradictions of Christians within the universal Church.

In Latin America there is arising, not from theological discussions (necessary for reflection), but from the actual life of the peoples, a new face of the Church: poor, prophetic, witnessing; a sign of hope, in the grass-roots Church communities, of a first liberating step towards becoming aware that the kingdom of God is a concrete thing, and that justice consists in re-establishing the disrupted brotherhood of man and sharing bread and freedom in truth with our brothers.

These testimonies are the signs that in some way indicate this search for justice and this path of peace as the fundamental value of life.

Norbert Mette

Between the 'Security Society' and the Peace Movement— On the Current Debate Among Catholics in the Federal Republic of Germany

'With particular regard to current political questions *Pax Christi* urges people to work for deliberate, unilateral steps towards disarmament on the part of the NATO Western Alliance. This would inspire trust in the Warsaw Pact States and elicit corresponding disarmament measures, which in turn would lead to a comprehensive disarmament agreement. The legitimate need for security on all sides must be taken into account.'

'Today voices are raised in support of unilateral disarmament, even if only to set an example. We believe that this attitude threatens the peace, autonomy and freedom of our peoples. Yet we are absolutely united in calling loudly and clearly for everything possible to be done to avoid the use of the weapons available today.'

THESE TWO quotations are taken from statements issued almost simultaneously—in June 1982—to the people of the Federal German Republic. Both of them originate in Catholic circles and, as is quite clear, each takes up a particular stance in the current peace debate. The first question is drawn from a declaration in which the German Section of *Pax Christi* called on all Christians to organise Peace Weeks in autumn 1982. In this it was following the lead given by the Evangelical project 'Sign of reconciliation—ministry of peace' (*Sühnezeichen/Friedensdienst*).[1] The second quotation comes from a joint declaration of the French and German bishops entitled 'For Peace'.[2] Neither of these statements attracted much attention in the media of the Federal Republic. Only the conservative-oriented press reacted with visible relief to find that official government policy was still supported by the Catholic bishops; at present the Evangelical Church here is felt to be a less reliable partner.[3]

The two quotations are adduced because they are characteristic of the current debate in the Catholic Church in the Federal Republic on the related questions of

67

'security, disarmament and peace'. Not only do they show that serious differences of opinion exist with regard to concrete ways of ensuring peace; one can no longer speak of a united front in German Catholicism with regard to peace and security policies, such as was presented to the 'outside world' in the fifties and sixties. More than this, the two declarations illustrate the diverse approaches with which Catholics attempt to participate in the general debate on constructive peace-politics, beginning by seeking to influence public opinion within the Church. Very roughly three positions and modes of argument can be distinguished at the moment:[4]

1. In its Peace Week 1982 declaration *Pax Christi* was consistently pursuing the course upon which it set out with its manifesto 'Disarmament and Security' ratified at the end of 1980.[5] In its preamble we read: 'With this manifesto *Pax Christi* is taking a stand on an issue which has become one of survival for all mankind. It is not claimed to be the only one. It is one of several which in all good faith are trying to find solutions and procedures to ensure and promote peace. It is an attempt to give an ethically based and practical answer to the current problems of disarmament and security, taking as its starting-point the declarations of the Second Vatican Council and the General Synod of the bishops of the Federal Republic. It needs continual reassessment. *Pax Christi* will re-examine and develop this manifesto at the Assembly of Delegates in 1982.'

Thus *Pax Christi* enters the current debate on peace policies by pointing out the most urgent issues and problems and helping people to find their way in this area and thus form their own judgment. It provides analyses and information (e.g., alternatives to the existing policies of security and deterrents), establishes ethical criteria and adopts definite positions on some questions (e.g., its condemnation of arms exports, its rejection of the NATO double resolution) and develops concrete political perspectives (e.g., opting for a gradualist strategy in arms reduction). The aim is to encourage a greater sensitivity in questions of ensuring peace and of disarmament, particularly among the churchgoing public, in parishes, groups and societies, which constitute a considerable factor in forming the ethical and political will; by creating an 'informed awareness of the disarmament issue' it is intended to work towards a change in security priorities by majority vote in party and government.

Pax Christi claims to base its own position on the gospel of peace and to be trying to put it into effect in the present social and political environment. At the same time it is made clear that, with regard to practical ways of ensuring peace, Christians may have differing views, and that those who responsibly put forward a position other than that of *Pax Christi* are to be respected. This approach, taking committed action on behalf of one's own convictions, without morally disqualifying one's opponents but engaging them in honest argument, is characteristic of the way one section of German Catholics participates in the peace debate. It is an approach followed by a number of other groups, including *(a)* the *German Catholic Youth Federation* (BDKJ), which has adopted the motto 'Peace and Justice' for its work in the immediate future, and has formulated a number of 'starting-points' calling among other things for a re-orientation of peace and security policies;[6] *(b)* the *Bensberg Circle*, an association of independent Christians which made itself heard in August 1982 by issuing another notable *Memorandum*, urging two things as the first step towards multilateral disarmament, namely, gradual unilateral reduction of atomic weapons and at the same time the remodelling of conventional defence along the lines of defensive weaponry;[7] *(c)* the movement entitled *Christians Against Atomic Weapons*, which regards the use of atomic weapons as intrinsically un-Christian and rejects them absolutely.[8]

The approach of these groups is not without its difficulties: there is controversy in their own ranks as well as between the groups themselves as to how radical such Christian-motivated peace initiatives should be and how far they should go in their concrete political demands. Pacts with groups in the Peace Movement which hold aloof from faith or even oppose it are disputed issues. But no doubt the greatest difficulty is that of maintaining what has been called a 'committed tolerance' towards the majority of members of any church who must be regarded as uncritical supporters of what the *Pax Christi* manifesto calls the *security society*, that society which gives priority to military ideas of security. It has happened that young people wanting to hold a peace service have been refused permission; that Catholics involved in ecumenical peace circles are either not listened to in their own parishes or are pushed to the fringe; that full-time church workers get into difficulties with their superiors when they propagate Vatican statements on peace and disarmament or speak in favour of them; all these may be isolated cases but they are not untypical of the experience of peace workers in the Catholic area.

2. Another mode of Catholic participation in the peace debate can be seen in the recent declarations of the Catholic bishops of the Federal Republic.[9] The bishops regard themselves as specifically responsible for pointing out the indispensable principles for any peace which is worthy of mankind. So long as there is no fundamental discrepancy between these maxims and the ruling political concepts of peace and security, there is no reason, in their view, for the Christian to refuse his assent to official policies, regardless of the fact that he may be of a different view. It can be no surprise, therefore, that the bishops' documents are much clearer in drawing the boundaries of legitimate action on the part of the Peace Movement than they are when it comes to the effects of the prevailing policies of security and deterrent (see the quotation at the beginning of this article).

Just as the bishops claim a special ethical competence in the present debate, they attribute a special political competence to the politicians. This is why they prefer to influence the ethical and political will 'from above'; what comes 'from below' is suspected of being emotional, irrelevant and one-sided.

It would not be entirely right, however, to accuse the bishops of uncritically supporting the *status quo*; their statements contain clear demands for more thoroughgoing efforts in this area: for instance in the joint declaration of the French and German bishops the arms race is described as a terrible threat to life; they insist that there be 'a systematic attempt to reach agreement on controlled arms limitation'; that the balance of power should not be seen as depending merely on weapon potential, but that other factors should be taken into account; that 'the others' situation must be understood, their call for security must be heard and their fears taken seriously'. It is noteworthy that in his address to the German Bishops' Conference Cardinal Höfner asserts that a war raged with modern technological weapons (an ABC war) would unleash gigantic and uncontrollable destruction and would far exceed the levels of just defence. Even though, when one reads the documents, these and similar declarations do not strike one very forcibly and, in part, cannot be interpreted in one sense only, they do show that the German bishops have not totally ignored the continuing development of the papal teaching on peace and disarmament, although they may not have given such single-minded attention to it as the bishops and bishops' conferences of other countries. But at least they provide a link for further possibilities. There can be no fundamental objection to Catholic groups joining in this work and contributing to the formation of public opinion within the Church. In their more clear-cut line they cannot be actually recognised by the bishops, but all the same they can regard themselves as tolerated.

3. This more nuanced evaluation of the bishops' approach is all the more appropriate since it forestalls the attempts being made by influential circles within the Catholic Church in the Federal Republic to re-establish a unified line in the name of so-called 'German Catholicism' with regard to peace and security policies, and to commit its members once more to that uniformity which—with certain exceptions— made it a dependable and manageable partner of the government at the time of the

rearmament and atomic weapons debate in the fifties and sixties. Those who support this position—as was evident at the time—manifest an intolerance towards their opponents; almost any means is justifiable in getting rid of those who threaten the supposed consensus in their own ranks.[10]

This attitude was recently exemplified in the resolution entitled 'On the present peace debate', adopted in November 1981 by the plenary assembly of the Central Committee of German Catholics (ZdK), the official forum of the associations and institutions of the lay apostolate in the Catholic Church in the Federal German Republic. This document takes up an isolated and extreme position among the various points of view of the churches in the Federal Republic.[11] The Memorandum of the *Bensberg Circle* gives examples of how far this Central Committee document has departed from more recent papal peace ethics: 'Basically the Central Committee passes an exclusively negative judgment on the other side in the conflict; the Vatican documents do not, and warn others against doing so. The Central Committee justifies the policies of the one side right up to the actual decision to increase armaments; the Vatican concentrates on a critique of the policies of both sides. The Central Committee supports the policies of deterrent; the Vatican sees through the fateful implications of these policies of distrust and calls for a turning away from the deterrent mentality. The Central Committee bends all its ideas towards the consolidation of Western security policies even among the civilian population; the pope appeals for peace efforts and a readiness to take risks in policies of trust and for the mobilisation of the potential for reconciliation of the Christian community.' Faced with such an attitude it follows that any questioning of the prevailing political and military concepts of security will meet not only with total lack of understanding but also with summary accusations. It is plain how uncompromising the Central Committee is in pursuing its reinforcement of existing political conditions when those of its members who put forward different views are disqualified as having a mistaken (*sic*) view of what constitutes the threat to peace.[12]

Summing up, we can say that in the Federal Republic of Germany the new Peace Movement is also being actively supported and promoted by groups and parishes of the Catholic Church. They are only a minority in this Church; the prevailing attitude can perhaps be termed the 'fear of getting involved'. There is no doubt that German Catholics value peace highly; but, as it was aptly put in the resolution on 'Development and Peace' at the General Synod of the Bishops of the Federal Republic in 1975, they prefer to see it as a 'secure system containing as few conflicts as possible'.[13] The factors which have led to this mentality are manifold and cannot be analysed here.[14] In any case the peace debate is in fact running counter to any such need for harmony. The Catholic Church cannot withdraw from the debate; but the majority feel that it is not really native to it; it is an issue forced on the Catholic Church 'from outside'. Correspondingly, as we have shown, official pronouncements evince a moderate reserve rather than the readiness to contribute in a committed way to the formation of public awareness and public opinion. Some of those who do try to work for peace among their own ranks on the basis of genuine principles experience huge obstacles and have to fight against prejudice and defamation. Thus at the moment a great deal of energy is absorbed by the struggle within the Church over the proper mode of participation in the peace debate. Naturally this inhibits the mobilisation of that peace potential which, as the Synod resolution expressed it, is of the Church's very nature.

It is a fact that the Catholic Church in the Federal Republic is coming under increasing pressure. Compared with the Evangelical Church in the Federal Republic and with the Catholic churches of other countries, the way in which it is restricted by its involvement with the prevailing concept of security policy is somewhat strange. It threatens to lose touch with the new evaluation in the theology and ethics of peace which is taking place in Catholic circles and even more so in ecumenical ones. This acts increasingly as an irritant among the Catholic population. Even if we can hardly expect a rapid change in the deeply-rooted attitudes and thought-patterns, these very insecurities mean that there is a chance for a learning process.

Translated by Graham Harrison

Notes

1. Text in *Frankfurter Rundschau* 23.6.1982
2. Text in *Herder-Korrespondenz 36* (1982) 385-387.
3. See H.-J. Benedict 'Auf dem Weg zur Friedenskirche? Entstehung und Erscheinungsformen der neuen Friedensbewegung in der evangelischen Kirche' in *Die neue Friedensbewegung (Friedensanalysen 16)* (Frankfurt 1982) pp. 227-244.
4. See also L. Lemhöfer 'Zögernde Aufbruch aus dem Kalten Krieg. Die katholische Kirche und die bundesdeutche "neue Friedensbewegung" ' in *ibid*, pp. 245-257; J. Harms 'Modelle und Aktionen für Abrüstung aus den Kirchen' in *Frieden–Abrüstung–Sicherheit* ed. H. Schierholz (Reinbek 1981) pp. 258-266.
5. See *Abrüstung und Sicherheit. Plattform der Pax Christi (Dokumentation Kirche und Abrüstung IV)* (Frankfurt 1981).
6. See H. Missalla 'Die "Startpositionen Frieden und Gerechtigkeit" des BDKJ' in *KatBl 107* (1982) 447-451.
7. See *Frieden—für Katholiken eine Provokation? Ein Memorandum* ed. Bensberger Kreis (Reinbek 1982).
8. See *Atomrüstung—christlich zu verantworten?* ed. A. Battke (Düsseldorf 1982). This list of peace groups in Catholic circles is not meant to be exhaustive. For instance besides the BDKJ one ought to make separate mention of some of its member associations (KJG, KSG, etc.). Then there are the student parishes and their federation, the Study Group of Catholic Student and University Parishes (AGG). Catholics also work in the movement 'Life without Armaments' which arose in Evangelical circles. Furthermore numerous local and regional groups and movements have sprung up. More than 100 Catholic groups (totalling about 300 signatories) signed the 'Church from Below' declaration at the peace demonstration in Düsseldorf on 4 September 1982.
9. As well as the declaration 'For Peace' (note 2), see the declaration and the press report of the Spring Plenary Assembly of the German Bishops' Conference in *Frieden und Sicherheit. Arbeitshilfen 21* (Bonn, no date) 5-10; J. Cardinal Höffner *Das Friedensproblem im Licht des christlichen Glaubens. Vortrag zur Eröffnung der Vollversammlung der Deutschen Bischofskonferenz Fulda, 21.9.1981* (Bonn, no date).
10. See the brief accounts in P. Engelhardt 'Die Lehre vom "gerechten Krieg" in der vorreformatorischen und katholischen Tradition' in *Der gerechte Krieg: Christentum, Islam, Marxismus (Friedensanalysen 12)* (Frankfurt 1980) pp. 72-124, esp. 104-111; L. Lemhöfer, in the article cited in note 4.
11. Texts in *Herder-Korrespondenz 35* (1981) 624-630. See W. Huber 'Die Kirchen und der Friede' in *Abermals: Kampf dem Atomtod* (Frankfurter Hefte, suppl. 4) (Frankfurt 1982) pp. 119-130, and Th. Risse-Kappen *Analyse und synoptische Dokumentation von Stellungnahmen aus den Kirchen in der Bundesrepublik Deutschland* (Bonn 1982).
12. This happened to representatives of the BDKJ. See *Frankfurter Rundschau* 8.2.1982.
13. 'Der Beitrag der katholischen Kirche in der Bundesrepublik Deutschland für Entwicklung und Frieden' in *Gemeinsame Synode der Bistümer in der Bundesrepublik Deutschland. Offizielle Gesamtausgabe I* (Freiburg 1976) pp. 459-510, esp. p. 496.
14. There are illuminating hypotheses in the *Memorandum* of the *Bensberg Circle* (note 7). See also Th. Risse/H. J. Möller 'Zum Stand der kirchlichen Friedensarbeit' in *Frieden in Sicherheit* ed. N. Glatzel/E. J. Nagel (Freiburg 1981) pp. 176-212.

Edward Schillebeeckx

Eager to Spread the Gospel of Peace

HOW CAN Christians, together with the leaders of their churches, render a true account of the Gospel in a situation in which the nuclear armaments race can, because of its own inner logic, no longer be controlled and within the framework of a still prevalent ideology, which on the one hand requires an equilibrium of deterrents and the armaments spiral that is so closely connected with it and, on the other, encompasses continuing attempts to control armaments, but on the presupposition of this very equilibrium of deterrents?

This is the situation in which Christians are in fact living today. The churches are 'eager to spread the gospel of peace' (Eph. 6:15), but can they, with the prospect of a nuclear holocaust, influence States in any way in their political ideology of safety? Can they exert an influence both by political activity that is in accordance with that 'Gospel of peace' and by officially speaking as churches?

The Christian theologian who is sustained and inspired by the Gospel of peace cannot formulate any universal laws that will be valid at all times and in all places. He can, however, help in rendering an account of the hope that the Gospel of peace offers to us even in our present, apparently desperate historical situation. The really threatening aspect of the situation in which Christians are living today comes down essentially to this: Every party involved is trying to prevent war by threatening war and, what is more, by increasingly more destructive means. The old saying: *Si vis pacem, para bellum* holds good in our current situation—peace is only ensured by threatening war! In this article, I propose to limit my discussion of this ideology to the implications of this situation for Christians living in the atomic age.

1. AN OUTLINE OF THE PROBLEM

I shall not try to provide a comprehensive survey of the attitude found in the Old and New Testaments and in the Christian tradition that has resulted from this towards the reality of war. All that I can do here is to attempt to summarise in a few words the contents and conclusions of a number of historical studies of the question.[1]

(a) A Brief Survey

In the light of Jesus' own praxis of peace, New Testament Christianity was radically pacifist. Christians continued to be pacifists in their praxis until about the beginning of the fourth century. In AD 295, for example, the North African martyr Maximilian said: 'I cannot be a soldier; I am a Christian.' Long before this, Tertullian has already observed that Christians were present in barracks and, although he himself was the son of a centurion, he made an analogy between Christian baptism and the military standard oath and came to the conclusion that they were mutually exclusive. Soldiers who became Christians were eventually permitted to remain in the army, so long as they only carried out peaceful duties (that was possible at that time) and did not shed blood. The latter continued to be forbidden for Christian soldiers.

After the Constantinian and especially the Theodosian change, when the Christian Church took over the function of the Roman *religio* and became a State religion, Christians began to look for criteria by which they might distinguish between a 'just' and an 'unjust' war; they were only permitted to fight in a just war—and time and time again they presupposed that the wars which they actually waged were justified on this count.

It was precisely on this ideology that they theory of the 'just war' foundered. Although he probably did not intend to, Erasmus demonstrated that this theory was untenable in his well-known treatise, *Complaint of Peace.*[2] He may have been the first to do so and chose to seek refuge in the kingdom of inner peace, although even in his own heart he found discord. His ultimate conclusion was that peace could only be found in Jesus. In fact, his theory amounts to an important appeal to man's good will—impotent because it was precisely at this time that Machiavelli was writing his book about war, in which he claimed that war was necessary in order to preserve the power of the State, which lay outside the realm of ethics.

In more recent times, man's good will has become even more tightly enclosed within civil structures, which have in turn been shaped by a clearly defined economic structure. The ethos of peace that philosophers and theologians have attempted to elaborate has therefore come to an impasse formed by the inner logic of power structures.[3]

Since the Second World War, a teleological ethos of responsibility has been developed, above all in papal encyclicals, in which a theory has been evolved along the lines of earlier scholasticism. According to this theory, an action is judged to be good or bad on the basis of its inner relationship with the good or bad effect that is achieved by it. An action with an equally good and bad result is, in the light of this theory, given ethical approval, whereas an action which brings about a good result only *in* and *through* achieving a bad effect is ethically rejected without further ado.

On the basis of this theory, Popes John XXIII, Paul VI and John Paul II have declared all the aspects of the nuclear armaments race to be ethically impermissible, each pope stressing this more emphatically than his predecessor.[4] In the present pope's texts, it is not difficult to see that the language game of ethics has to some extent been abandoned now in favour of the language used in bearing witness to the Gospel, a language which transcends that of a purely ethical or juridical approach to the question. In my opinion, with this new evangelical approach we can, as Christians at least, really take up an evangelical position. Purely ethical and rational arguments can, after all, always be made impotent by hostile reasoning, man's unredeemed free will and the logic and ideology of the secular policy of power.

(b) Right and Wrong Questions

But bearing witness evangelically can also be made impotent. This bearing witness may, for example, be too abstract, the evangelical 'peace of Jesus' being simply contrasted with the peace that men are hoping to obtain by means of a strategy of deterrence. There is, after all, a kind of evangelical pacifism which simply leaves the ideological policy of safety followed by sovereign States as it is and does no more than

F

merely present the radical criticism of the Gospel in contrast to it. This is acting as though even a Christian leader of the State is able to act as a free person who is not deeply immersed in the structural complexity of a tough political, economic and social system.

In opposition to this, I would claim that radical evangelical resistance to specific violence and certainly also to the nuclear armament spiral must be resistance of a kind that is given a historical form in the political activity of Christians in this world. It is only if this happens that the 'Gospel of peace' will avoid becoming a Utopian or a purely eschatological longing and will in fact begin at least to renew, to some extent, the face of the earth.

On the other hand, however, there are Christians who regard this radically evangelical opposition to the possession and possible use of nuclear weapons as a symptom of decadent anxiety. They reproach others for apparently not knowing what it will cost not only to live but also to die for it, if need be with resistance based on nuclear weapons. The culture and economy of the West on the one hand and of the communist world on the other are the values for which men will risk a nuclear war. Christians believe them: 'nothing can separate us from God' and 'nothing can happen to us' and some claim that fear of an atomic war is evidence of a decadent culture that no longer knows what it is living for. This mysticism is often used in order to approve, either secretly or even openly, of nuclear armament, at least by what is always called the 'good party', because the fact that it is always necessary to have more and more nuclear weapons is, according to this way of thinking, always the other person's, the enemy's fault. On both sides—and very soon it will be on all sides—it is always claimed that justice and great human values are being served!

The danger that is present in this mythical surrender is that it is too early. This Christian mysticism is based on the unarmed and disarming impotence of the strength that comes from the 'peace of Christ' which is 'not of this world' and is therefore rightly contradictory to every reduction of the coming kingdom of God to the level of purely human and political planning for the future. It is, however, often regarded by Christians as setting the political activity of ethically good people who are really concerned with true humanity outside the sphere of the kingdom of God.

It is, of course, true to say that the kingdom of God is not the same as a just and sound economy, but there is no doubt that it is directly concerned with it! Christians are therefore confronted with the urgent question as to how they can influence the decisions made by the leaders of their sovereign States, not simply by making moral appeals (which those leaders may appear to treat with politeness, but in fact usually ignore, often rudely or with irritation), but in fact by engaging in specific political action. Otherwise, it is easy to explain war as a kind of natural disaster that is beyond man's control, as a bio-historical necessity in the process of man's evolution or as a misfortune, due to original sin, occurring in human history.

We should therefore never forget that the Christian proclamation of the redemption brought about in and through Jesus Christ has greater power (although that is often exercised in human impotence). As Thomas Aquinas said: 'The power of grace is more abundant than that of original sin.' It would seem that this mystical attitude is forgetful of this principle! The question that arises in this context is, of course, whether we are able and really want to take hold of this superior power of grace in our political action and how we can do this.

The fact is, after all, self-evident: There has been war throughout the whole history of man and men and the whole of creation have been disfigured and destroyed. What is more, Christians have also played an important part in this process. It was for a very good reason that the Bible projected this historical knowledge of man's experience (a struggle between nomads and settled people that remained alive in the memory of the

Israelites) back to an incident in the earliest history of the people: the Cain and Abel story (Gen. 4).

The existence of only two brothers living side by side—the first brothers in the world, according to this literary genre—led to fratricide. It is also clear from this story that this is forbidden by God. Whether one fellow-man is killed with a primitive cudgel or whether millions are killed by nuclear rockets, their environment being destroyed at the same time, both events are, despite the extremely dramatic difference between them, from the ethical point of view or, as the Christians would say, from God's point of view, equally impermissible, inhuman and anti-divine, so much so that the Christians can have no part in them.

At the same time, however, we must remember the fact that the concern for the inviolability of even one person is enhanced by the experience of mass murders that go beyond the imagination. It would seem that it is the anonymity of the blood-bath that draws our attention to the individual. There is, then, a qualitative difference between a single act of fratricide and a nuclear holocaust. This is probably the real point of the story of Cain and Abel.

Kant may, because of the bourgeois society and the period in which he was living, have formulated his famous ethical imperative as the only possibility and strategy by which one's *own* safety could be protected. Nonetheless, his principle remains valid: 'Act so that you always use humanity both in your own person and in the other's person as an end and never as a means.' This principle can be interpreted a little differently in the following way: It is possible to fail oneself with regard to one's own rights, but not with regard to another's rights and his or her inviolability.

Seen in this light of a refusal to treat one's fellow-man as an instrument, torture can never, for example, be justified by the value of the information that it may yield. Yet it is done by all States when the need arises and even by Christians. In a political system of power—and politics are in the concrete always a power game (even though that power may not in itself involve violence)—moral demands and appeals, made by anyone at all, even a pope, only play a small and usually insignificant part. In the politics of 'this world', it is always the concrete effect or the success of certain actions with regard to the concrete power structures that has the last word. The Gospel subjects these power structures, on the basis of their political economy, to the radical criticism of the sole kingdom or humanity of the one God, but the rhetorical pathos caused by the Word of God does not in itself change the politics of this world.

The right question to ask in the concrete, then, is: How can and probably how must we, as Christians, act politically in the light of our faith in the Gospel of peace and, what is more, act in such a way that as a result of that political action there will in fact be no nuclear war? The realistic but apparently despairing point of departure is that the nuclear weapons of that war are unfortunately already with us. How can and must we act, then, so that the powerful States not only do not use these weapons, but also in fact simply destroy them and, what is more, preferably without a nuclear war having any chance of success, because of our radical evangelical activity?

I use the word 'preferably' because, if, despite everything, it still comes to the point where we have nuclear war, the Christian may then—and only then—say that 'nothing can separate us from the love that God has shown in Jesus'. Jesus, the peacemaker, was himself reduced to silence on the cross, but the community of believers who confess that he is Lord know, in the light of their faith in the resurrection, that he was, despite this, raised by God to be Lord of history. Power can be triumphant in impotence.

I would therefore agree with certain specialists in political science that the essential question (even for Christians) is: What is the best strategy to ensure that a war with nuclear weapons (which are already with us) and finally war as such is outlawed? I would also defend their standpoint that it is only if weapons can in fact be dispensed with in politics that they will also be thrown in great numbers on the scrap-heap and eventually completely disappear and that the way to military détente is therefore bound to be through political détente.

Political détente can, however, only be brought about when political, material and spiritual values are no longer concentrated in a few places, but are more justly distributed among the whole of mankind. The slogan: 'Get rid of nuclear weapons from the world' would seem, now that those nuclear weapons are already with us, to be within reach of becoming a reality in the political sense only when relationships are more just throughout the whole of the world and especially when a just economic system, one that does not make the rich richer by making the poor poorer, is established worldwide. Political pressure and protest of all kinds by Christians as well (and especially by Christians) must therefore first and foremost be directed at the prevailing unjust political economy and the present concentration of power that is the result of it.

It is not possible to dissociate the autonomous rationality of the armaments race from this political and economic complex. We are therefore bound to ask whether the Christian ought, in the 'meantime', to be resigned to the fact that there is a spiral of nuclear armament? Can he or she do no more than directly proclaim the message of the Gospel in a loud voice? What is certain from the evangelical point of view is that he or she cannot collaborate in this arms race, which in itself costs, both in the East and in the West, millions of human lives already in the starving Third World (even if the weapons themselves are never used). The politicians who favour a policy of safety, both those in the East and those in the West, have only two words to say to this: Too bad! This is because on both sides the ideology prevails that 'the other side is to blame; we are not to blame—we only want justice and true freedom', each side coloured according to its own understanding of justice.

Is this, then, the correct way of expressing the question: We have nuclear weapons with us already; what, then, is the best strategy, given this situation? In my view, this is only half of the truth. The fundamental truth of the situation is to be found in the possession itself of these weapons. In view of the fact that the strategy of deterrence ('on both sides') is meaningless and ineffectual without a readiness also to use these weapons if need be, this deterrence is itself, on the basis of the will to use the weapons, a threat to mankind, inhuman and ethically unjustifiable. Christians may not be naïve, but they may also not conclude a pact with 'this world'.

This concrete situation, however, results in one urgent question that Christians are bound to ask: Can we passively look on while these nuclear weapons are possessed and positioned? Even in the case of nuclear self-defence, what will be left of that 'self'? And what are the values that are to be defended in accordance with truth?[5]

In the course of the debate about steps to be taken on the way to unilateral disarmament, Harrie Kuitert has said: 'Ethics without politics are as dangerous as politics without ethics' and others have echoed him in the Netherlands. I am completely in agreement with this statement. Kuitert has also added to this: 'unless we allow the result to count as the ultimately determining factor'.[6] This result is, of course, the fact that there will be no nuclear war. Kuitert calls this a roundabout way, but that is something that we learn from the realism of experience. In the world as it in fact is—what Scripture calls 'this world'—it is the right of the most powerful that prevails. Even though an evangelical protest is diametrically opposed to such a political Darwinism and Machiavellianism, Christians are bound, in their efficient political activity, to take it into account. Even in the medieval world, which was dominated by the Christian Church, things were not radically different. We have always to be extremely suspicious of 'power'.

Efficient activity in this case means, of course, acting in such a way that there will in fact be no nuclear war. The apparently despairing aspect of this problem is, however, this: One group (including the Christian members of it) maintains that (in view of the fact that there are nuclear weapons) the intended result, in other words, the prevention of war, can only be efficiently assured by the possession of nuclear weapons, at least if there is a balance of power between both potential parties opposing one another. The other group (again including the Christians who belong to it), on the other hand, claim that it is this system of deterrents in itself and therefore the very possession of nuclear weapons which forms the greatest danger of nuclear war and that this danger increases in probability as the number of States possessing those weapons grows (although the political assumption is always made that one's own leaders have more common sense than the leaders of other States).

Neither of these two affirmations can at present be verified, because the only atomic bombs that have in fact been used were dropped at a time when only one country possessed them and the enemy country was therefore defenceless. What, however, are we to say if both countries are more or less equal in strength? Which of the two would venture to use a nuclear weapon? The fact is that neither side of this dilemma can as yet be proved true or false. The critical question, then, is: How can the result (the fact that there will be no nuclear war) be discounted as the ultimately determining factor? Or is an attitude of resignation the only possible one—an attitude of waiting until nuclear war comes or does not come—in order to see which of the two affirmations is really valid? Surely something is not right here!

2. THE PRAXIS OF THE GOSPEL TRANSLATED INTO POLITICAL ACTION

First in our modern bourgeois society in the West and then also in the countries of the Eastern Bloc, religion has been relegated to spheres in which it is unable to oppose the State's policy of safety and its resulting economic conflict. The Gospel has, in other words, become interiorised and excluded from the sphere of public political activity.

Society cannot be traced back to the sum total of individual actions, nor can the individual be traced back to the sum total of social relationships. Societies—and this includes sovereign States—have always developed into what they are at a given time and they have usually developed, what is more, in a way that neither side concerned has foreseen, intended, planned or carried out. Many social processes have relative autonomy with regard to the people who set them in motion and shape them. They have a structured course of development. Nonetheless, it is human beings who, for example, wage war and they do so by their actions. These structures also form the personality structure of the individuals in any given society.

This cultural and anthropological situation throws some light on the question why a mere appeal to people's consciences or to their good will and even bearing witness evangelically in the form of proclamation so often simply rebounds from the wall formed by those tough structures. This happens above all in the case of the modern 'structurally a-theistic' social structures that are to be found in all spheres of public life: economics, politics, armed military defence, the law and the natural and human sciences. What, then, is the task confronting the Christian who does not want to live apart from 'this world' in a sacred ghetto?

What made the Jews say about Jesus: 'He taught them as one who had authority' (Matt. 7:29)? The answer to this question can be found in the whole of the New Testament: In the way in which he turns to man, Jesus makes it immediately clear what he is talking about and also proves it to be true. He does not, for example, say to Zacchaeus, the little man in the tree: 'God loves you', as the modern fundamentalist posters displayed in railway stations and elsewhere in the Netherlands would have us believe. On the contrary, he goes to Zacchaeus' home, eats and drinks with him and proves by his action and by his concern for his fellow-man the truth that God loves him.

Jesus' message was therefore so integrated into his active and communicative appearance that his proclamation and the praxis of his life interpreted each other mutually, with the result that together, proclaiming and acting, they also changed situations in the concrete and he was able, in this world, to anticipate the completion of the kingdom of God. Bearing witness evangelically is therefore only a part of a concrete evangelical activity in the world and only that whole radiates power and achieves something in this world. The same also applies to Christians in their *sequela Jesu* or following of Jesus. The community of believers is not only required to make a confession, but also to have a praxis that is in accordance with the kingdom of God, although that praxis must be within the conditions of 'this world'.

In modern situations, in which man has come to believe that society in the concrete is not an 'order established by God' or purely the result of human planning, but also a system resulting from actions that are both intended and not intended, this connection between bearing witness evangelically by proclamation and the Christian praxis of life also has a political dimension. In addition to an interpersonal turning towards one's fellow-men, this 'turning' is also translated into political action and influencing social, political and economic structures in such a way that these structures do not in the long run make one group whole and bring salvation to that group while destroying other groups. This 'turning' also takes the form of working for a good and just society.

The 'peace of God that passes all understanding' (Phil. 4:7) and social peace in the world cannot be divided. Even though one is not identical with the other, they belong together. From the theological point of view therefore, even though it may be in the fragmentary state of 'this world', there must be an inner and positive link between the 'peace of Christ' and the peace that is built up fragmentarily by human efforts and has to be built up again and again in the social and political sphere.

Not only some specialists in the field of political science but also those who are concerned with peace studies point from time to time (often not without a certain disdain) to 'another faculty' (by which they mean the faculty of theology) when they hear such words as 'the wolf dwelling with the lamb' and 'beating swords into ploughshares' (a way of speaking which certainly does not belong to the language of peace studies). It is true that the theologian cannot (on the condition that he has knowledge of what is being said by those who specialise in peace studies) dispense with this kind of language, the language of faith, but he must also be able to translate it into political action.

There is, after all, a form of theological reductionism, in which the aspect of grace contained in the power of the 'peace of Christ' is set alongside and even above the social, political and economic dimensions of human history, in so far as these achieve greater justice for all people (and, in view of their urgent plight, this means above all the least privileged) using the (non-violent) means of this world. It is true that the grace of the peace of Christ always transcends the forms in this world in which it appears, but it is equally true to say that that grace can only be found in the historical forms of this world, both in the forms in which political and social peace is extended throughout the world and in the inner 'peace' of man's heart. Such inner peace, however, in 'this world' takes the form of the broken state of inner grief caused by hostility between individuals, groups and nations killing and threatening to kill each other because of a desire to possess and retain. This inner peace therefore also directs the Christian's attention to the social, political and economic aspects of his world that are in need of change, salvation and reconciliation.

The transcendence of God and of faith in God cannot therefore, even in the case of the peace promised in the Gospel, be used as an excuse for political neutrality or for making a merely moral protest against the politics of power in this world. The peace of

Christ calls on Christians to develop and follow a theology of political praxis. The Christian cannot reduce the social and political reality of the world to its purely social and political components. There is much more involved than just this—man and his whole humanity in relationship with God are at stake. The Christian's political praxis, directed towards the building up of a society that is fitter for people to live in and is therefore free from war and the threat of war, is undoubtedly the social and political content of his Christian hope in terms of a historical praxis of peace.[7]

His policy of peace can therefore not be confined simply to appealing to and proclaiming evangelically the 'peace of Christ' and to condemning the nuclear arms race in the abstract. It calls also for many different political and practical translations of the Gospel of peace at the level of his own human history and that of his fellow-men. I will try to summarise what this means in the concrete in the concluding paragaphs of this section of my article.

Christians should avail themselves of the findings of recent peace studies and make a (non-ideological) analysis of the concrete structures of society in which 'war' appears as a phenomenon with many causes. In this, they should take into account the fact that modern sovereign States are becoming increasingly dependent on each other, with the result that the sovereignty of each State is at the same time becoming more and more limited. In addition to this, they should also bear in mind that the survival of a 'State' is, like its origins, very much of a chance event in history and therefore a matter of relative importance only.

It is also necessary for Christians to analyse the fact that this increasing 'world integration' is able to break the autonomous rationality of war. But the same phenomenon also implies a much greater concentration of power.

Together with others, Christians can also exert an influence on sovereign States with regard to their ideology of the policy of safety by voting and by their attitude towards the defence budget and taxation for defence projects. It is also very important for this ideology of the policy of safety to be analysed. The questions that have to be asked in this context are: Whose safety is involved? What is the State trying to make safe? And, most important of all, at whose cost?

An evangelical proclamation of the Gospel of peace that is at the same time wise will always point to the political dimension of being a Christian. The Christian also has to be educated as a Christian to work for peace, and catechesis at all levels has always to be concerned with the political dimension of faith. Finally, peace studies can also play an important part in forming the Christian's evangelical imagination, so that he can, together with others, develop new strategies. There is no doubt that the traditional models of thought have failed here.

This brings me to my last question: Will Christians, because of the evangelical demand (aided by the evangelical imagination), work positively, in their (always limited) political activity, for a strategy consisting of steps towards unilateral (nuclear) disarmament? Another contributor to this issue of *Concilium* thinks that this will not happen. It is, of course, true that men and women, including those who are Christians, are very divided in this question and often very emotional. I respect this difference of opinion.

3. A RISKY TRUST IN UNILATERAL NUCLEAR DISARMAMENT?

According to Jesus, a Christian may not enter into a pact with 'this world' and this teaching of Jesus and the whole of the New Testament becomes even more urgent in a world that is prepared to destroy one side completely in a limited or a total nuclear war (although we know from history that war becomes all the more probable as long as it remains limited; this is something that certain people think is possible in the case of a nuclear war). On the basis of this evangelical teaching, I feel obliged, as a Christian, to ask this question: Can the vicious circle of the (nuclear) arms race be broken in any way other than by the 'virtuous circle' of steps towards unilateral (nuclear) disarmament?

This risky trust in unilateral disarmament seems to me to provide an extreme possibility, but at the same time it would appear to be the only concrete possibility for anyone who really believes in Jesus as the Lord of history. All other means seem doomed to fail, even in principle, and we cannot wait until the world's goods are more justly distributed among people. It is, I believe, only on the basis of this risky trust that we can make an appeal to the mysticism of Christian surrender. Christians have, after all, learned from the fate of their crucified Lord that unarmed and disarming love is able to lead others to hit back in aggression (because the inner impotence of those others' outward policy of power is revealed in an irritating way by this love).

Do Christians really want to share in this possible fate? Or would they prefer to join in the game played by 'this world' or at least leave it as it is in a spirit of resignation? I believe that there are limits to the Christian's loyalty to the State in its policy of power and safety. This is something that we can learn from the New Testament. Leaving aside the details of a Christian strategy, I think that Christians should, in their political praxis, risk taking steps towards unilateral nuclear disarmament and that Church leaders should have the courage to point to the way of this evangelically 'risky trust' as one that we believers ought to follow. It is better for us to be martyrs because we refuse to help to prepare for a possible nuclear war than for us to be victims of such a war because we fail to oppose it actively. In martyrdom, the Christian thinks of himself and of others who also refuse to play the game. In becoming a victim, he thinks above all of the others who end as martyrs in a nuclear war.

I have, now at least, come to the conclusion that the way in which this evangelical decision, translated into a political course of steps towards unilateral nuclear disarmament, should be worked out in further detail cannot be formulated either directly or indirectly on the basis of the Gospel itself. It is simply not possible to derive even indirect criteria which will lead to a consensus of opinion among Christians from the Gospel concerning the concrete strategic details of the (necessary) steps that should be taken in the direction of unilateral disarmament. For this reason, the political work involved in unilateral disarmament has, I am now convinced, to be left to professional politicians, including Christian politicians who (are expert in the matter and who) are prepared to use their evangelical imagination in order to think of concrete political programmes.

Political programmes of this kind can never be completely covered by official pronouncements made by the churches as a detailed Christian translation of the evangelical demand for unilateral disarmament. In order to avoid any misunderstanding, perhaps I should express this idea in a more concrete way: The Gospel cannot provide either a direct or an indirect answer that is really meaningful to us in the twentieth century as to how these steps towards unilateral nuclear disarmament should be taken in detail, that is, whether we should aim to make Europe a nuclear-free zone or whether we should work towards establishing a nuclear-free zone in our own country or whether any other option should be our immediate aim. Because of this, our Church leaders should be more than simply cautious before giving concrete guide-lines here. This free political activity, however, is the inevitable consequence of an evangelical policy of peace which requires Christians to seek for politically meaningful and detailed possibilities by which steps may be taken in the direction of unilateral nuclear disarmament, which is an extreme and an urgent possibility which we should venture to trust.

If sovereign States and their ideological policy of safety are subjected in this way to the criticism of the Gospel and if Christians recognise from this the limits of their loyalty to the State to which they belong, then they will also be able to acknowledge the limits of their loyalty to that State's alliances within the Gospel. What is more, when these limits have been reached, Christians will therefore be able to act accordingly, although they will no doubt be aware of the fact that, in 'this world', they must expect persecution and imprisonment, as the early Christians did. The ultimate question, then, is not whether Christians are decadent and afraid of nuclear war, but rather whether they are ready to be martyred for 'man's affair', which is God's affair. It is only if they are prepared for this that 'God's affair' can really be made credible in the eyes of the world.

Translated by David Smith

Notes

See, for example, J. Blank *Orientierung* 46 (1982) 14-15, 157-163; 19, 213-216; 20, 220-223; A. Alföldi *Studien zur Geschichte der Weltkrise des 3. Jahrhunderts nach Christus* (Darmstadt 1967); *Der gerechte Krieg: Christentum, Islam, Marxismus* (Frankfurt 1980) ed. R. Steinweg; *Das Evangelium des Friedens* (Munich 1982) ed. P. Eicher; R. Spaemann *Zur Kritik der politischen Utopie* (Stuttgart 1977) pp. 77-103.

2. Erasmus *Querela pacis undique gentium eiectae profligataeque. Ausgewählte Schriften* ed. W. Welzig (Darmstadt 1968) 5, pp. 359-451.

3. P. Juganaru *L'Apologie de la guerre dans la philosophie contemporaine* (Paris 1933); M. Walzer *Just and Unjust Wars. Amoral Argument with Historical Illustrations* (New York 1977); D. Senghaas *Friedensforschung und Gesellschaftskritik* (Munich 1970); R. Aron *Penser la guerre* (Paris 1976) I and II; H. Schrey 'Fünzig Jahre Besinnung über Krieg und Frieden' *Theologische Rundschau* 43 (1978) 201-229 and 266-284; 46 (1981) 58-96 and 149-180. See also E. Schillebeeckx, T. Beemer and J. A. van der Ven 'Theologen over kernontwapening' *Tijdschrift voor Theologie* 21 (1981) 3; *Wetenschap en vrede* (24 in the series published by the Centre for Peace Studies, Nijmegen) 7 (1982) 3.

4. See M. D. Chenu *La Doctrine sociale d l'Eglise comme idéologie* (Paris 1979); *Kirche und Kernbewaffnung* ed. H. O. Kirckhoff (Neukirchen and Vluyn) 1981.

5. B. Paskins and M. Dockrill *The Ethics of War* (London 1979) pp. 61ff.

6. H. Kuitert in the Dutch daily paper *Trouw* (28 and 30 September 1982).

7. E. Schillebeeckx 'Op zoek naar de heilswaarde van een politieke vredespraxis', 'Theologen over kernontwapening' in *Tijdschrift voor Theologie* cited in note 3, 232-244.

Contributors

JOSEPH COMBLIN was born in Brussels in 1923 and was ordained in 1947. He has exercised his ministry in Latin America since 1958, principally in Brazil, Ecuador and Chile, where he is currently serving. He has also taught in the Faculty of Theology of the Catholic University of Louvain since 1971, and has been a visiting professor at the Harvard Divinity School. His works on the theology of peace (*Théologie de la Paix*) and of revolution (*Théologie de la révolution*) have been translated into a number of languages. One of his latest works is *The Church and the National Security State* (Maryknoll (NY) 1979).

MIGUEL D'ESCOTO is a Maryknoll priest, who was the founder of Orbis Press. He has also worked in Chile in the whole field of social development and was personally very much involved in the revolutionary process of Nicaragua. He is presently Minister of the Exterior of Nicaragua.

ADOLFO PÉREZ ESQUIVEL was born in Buenos Aires on 26 November 1931. He studied at the Escuela Nacional de Bellas Artes at Buenos Aires and La Plata, ending his studies as lecturer in sculpture in 1956, during which year he married a musical artist, a composer, with whom he has had three children. He has lectured in various national universities and institutes, and taken part in exhibitions, obtaining various prizes and honours. Sculpture and drawing have also been a means for him to express his feelings on injustice and the long pilgrimage of the people in search of liberation.

In 1971 he joined Gandhian groups; he quickly became a leading member and helped in a plan for an urban community. He elaborated his own inner preparation more profoundly, based on the Gospel and on the contributions offered by non-violence. In 1973 he founded the journal *Paz y Justicia* and the Service for Latin American Non-Violent Action. The journal was later adopted as the press organ of the Justice and Peace Service. In the same year the Conference on Non-Violent Strategy for Latin American Liberation took place in Medellín, Colombia. It was the second meeting of organisations and groups working for justice using non-violent methodology. At this event Pérez Esquivel was nominated General Co-ordinator of the Service for Latin America.

He also participated in the creation and development in Argentina of the Co-ordinating Service for Christian Bodies and Organisations (CEOC); he supports the Ecumenical Movement for Human Rights (MEDH) and is a founding member of the Permanent Assembly for Human Rights (APDH). On 4 April 1977 he was arrested and placed in the custody of the National Executive Powers, by decree No. 929 of 4 April 1977, remaining in detention until 1978 and then in a situation of 'supervised freedom' until the end of 1979. In 1980 he was awarded the Nobel Peace Prize which he received 'on behalf of the peoples of Latin America and in a very special way of my brothers, the poorest and smallest, for these are the most loved by God'.

FRANÇOIS HOUTART was born in 1929 in Brussels and is a priest of the Malines-Brussels diocese. He holds a doctorate in sociology and a diploma in town-planning and a higher degree from the University of Chicago. He is a professor at the Catholic University of Louvain, director of the university's centre for socio-religious research and editor of the international sociology of religion journal *Social Compass*. He has carried out research in the sociology of religion and developmental sociology in several countries, notably the USA, Latin America, Sri Lanka, India, Vietnam and Tanzania. His writings include *Aspects sociologiques du catholicisme américain* (Paris 1957), *Eglise et Révolution en Amérique Latine* (Tournai and Paris 1964), *Church and Revolution* (New York 1970), *Religion and Ideology in Sri Lanka* (Colombo 1972), *Religion et modes de production précapitalistes* (Brussels 1970), with Geneviève Lemercinier, *Sociologie d'une commune vietnamienne* (Louvain-la-Neuve 1981).

MARY EVELYN JEGEN, SND, received her doctorate in medieval history from St Louis University, USA (1967). She has taught at the University of Dayton and the Pontifical Institute Regina Mundi (Rome), and is currently adjunct faculty at Creighton University and Mundelein College (USA) where she teaches postgraduate courses in Christian spirituality and social concerns. Currently she is national co-ordinator of *Pax Christi* USA and national chairperson of the American Fellowship of Reconciliation. She is co-editor of *The Earth Is the Lord's: Essays on Stewardship* (New York 1978) and *Growth with Equity: Strategies for Meeting Human Needs* (New York 1979). Among her most recent articles is 'Spirituality, Disarmament, and Security' *New Catholic World*, March/April 1982.

JOHN LINSKENS, CICM, was born in 1919 in Blitteswijck (Holland). In 1947 he was ordained to the priesthood in the Congregation of the Immaculate Heart of Mary (Scheut). He did his licentiate in theology at the Gregorian University in Rome in 1948 and his *ad lauream* at the Pontifical Institute in Rome in 1951. He taught New Testament and biblical languages from 1951-1957 in the theologiate of his congregation in Nijmegen and from 1957-1959 in Louvain (Belgium), after which he left for the Far East and taught New Testament in the Archdiocesan Seminary of Manila (Philippines) and in the East Asian Pastoral Institute (Ateneo University, Manila). Among his publications to be mentioned are: 'The Internal Structure of the Christian Community (Matt. 18)' in *St Louis Quarterly* (1965) 363-398 and 555-594, *St Louis Quarterly* (1966) 55-88 and (1966) 503-536; *The Foundational Experience of the Early Christian Movement* (San Antonio, Texas 1978); *Christ, Liberator of the Poor; Secularity, Wealth and Poverty in the Gospel of St Luke* (San Antonio, Texas 1976); *The Eucharist in the New Testament* (San Antonio, Texas 1979).

NORBERT METTE was born in 1946 and is married, with three children. He has published books and articles, and specialises in pastoral theology and religious education at the University of Münster. He is a spokesman of *Pax Christi* in the Diocese of Münster. His publications include *Theorie der Praxis* (1978), *Kirchlich distongierte Christlichkeit* (1982) and many articles on pastoral theology and the teaching of religion.

HEINRICH MISSALLA, born in 1926 in Wanne-Eickel, was ordained priest in 1953. He studied at Paderborn, Munich and Münster, gaining his doctorate of theology at the latter university in 1969. He is professor of practical theology and religious education at Essen. His works include: *Gott mit uns. Die deutsche katholische Kriegspredigt* (1968); *Weltbezogener Glaube. Analyse und Kritik der katechetischen Literatur für Berufs-schulen* (1968); *Für Volk und Vaterland. Die 'Kirchliche Kriegshilfe' im Zweiten Weltkrieg* (1978).

PAUL PEACHEY (PhD, Zurich, 1954) is associate professor of sociology, and co-ordinator of peace and world order studies at the Catholic University of America. He is co-ordinating a comparative international study on 'the residential areal bond', and is spending the 1982-1983 academic year at the University of Vienna (Austria) to join in the completion of the project. The first volume of reports from this study, of which he is the senior editor, will be published at the end of 1982 under the title, *The Residential Areal Bond: Local Attachments in Delocalized Societies* (New York). He has served in the international programme of the Mennonite Central Committee, and during the first half of the 1960s, as executive and study secretary of the Church Peace Mission, an association of Protestant peace societies. During that time he edited a volume entitled *Biblical Realism Confronts the Nation* (New York 1963).

EDWARD SCHILLEBEECKZ, OP, was born in Antwerp in Belgium in 1914 and was ordained in 1941. He studied at Louvain, Le Saulchoir, the Ecole des Hautes Etudes and the Sorbonne (Paris). He became a doctor of theology in 1951 and magister in 1959. Since 1958, he has been teaching dogmatic theology and hermeneutics at the University of Nijmegen (The Netherlands). He is editor-in-chief of the Dutch theological review *Tijdschrift voor Theologie*. His works in English translation include: *Christ the Sacrament of the Encounter with God* (New York 1963); *The Understanding of Faith* (London and New York 1974); *Jesus, an Experiment in Christology* (London and New York 1979); *Christ. The Experience of Jesus as Lord* (New York 1980) = *Christ. The Christian Experience in the Modern World* (London 1980); *Jesus and Christ. Interim Report on the Books Jesus and Christ* (London and New York 1980); *Ministry. Leadership in the Community of Jesus Christ* (New York 1981) = *Ministry. A Case for Change* (London 1981). In 1982 he was awarded the European Erasmus Prize for theology.

GORDON ZAHN is Professor Emeritus (sociology) at the University of Massachusetts-Boston. He has written *German Catholics and Hitler's Wars* (1962); *In Solitary Witness: The Life and Death of Franz Jaegerstaetter* (1964); *War, Conscience, and Dissent* (1964); *The Military Chaplaincy* (1969) *Another Part of the War: The Camp Simon Story* (1979). He is at present chairman of the Coordinating Committee of the *Pax Christi* USA Center on Conscience and War, Cambridge, Massachusetts.

CONCILIUM

The Church as Institution. Ed. Gregory Baum and Andrew Greeley. 0 8164 2575 2 168pp.

Politics and Liturgy. Ed. Herman Schmidt and David Power. 0 8164 2576 0 156pp.

Jesus Christ and Human Freedom. Ed. Edward Schillebeeckx and Bas van Iersel. 0 8164 2577 9 168pp.

The Experience of Dying. Ed. Norbert Greinacher and Alois Müller. 0 8164 2578 7 156pp.

Theology of Joy. Ed. Johannes Baptist Metz and Jean-Pierre Jossua. 0 8164 2579 5 164pp.

The Mystical and Political Dimension of the Christian Faith. Ed. Claude Geffré and Gustavo Guttierez. 0 8164 2580 9 168pp.

The Future of the Religious Life. Ed. Peter Huizing and William Bassett. 0 8164 2094 7 96pp.

Christians and Jews. Ed. Hans Küng and Walter Kasper. 0 8164 2095 5 96pp.

Experience of the Spirit. Ed. Peter Huizing and William Bassett. 0 8164 2096 3 144pp.

Sexuality in Contemporary Catholicism. Ed. Franz Bockle and Jacques Marie Pohier. 0 8164 2097 1 126pp.

Ethnicity. Ed. Andrew Greeley and Gregory Baum. 0 8164 2145 5 120pp.

Liturgy and Cultural Religious Traditions. Ed. Herman Schmidt and David Power. 0 8164 2146 2 120pp.

A Personal God? Ed. Edward Schillebeeckx and Bas van Iersel. 0 8164 2149 8 142pp.

The Poor and the Church. Ed. Norbert Greinacher and Alois Müller. 0 8164 2147 1 128pp.

Christianity and Socialism. Ed. Johannes Baptist Metz and Jean-Pierre Jossua. 0 8164 2148 X 144pp.

The Churches of Africa: Future Prospects. Ed. Claude Geffré and Bertrand Luneau. 0 8164 2150 1 128pp.

Judgement in the Church. Ed. William Bassett and Peter Huizing. 0 8164 2166 8 128pp.

Why Did God Make Me? Ed. Hans Küng and Jürgen Moltmann. 0 8164 2167 6 112pp.

Charisms in the Church. Ed. Christian Duquoc and Casiano Floristán. 0 8164 2168 4 128pp.

Moral Formation and Christianity. Ed. Franz Bockle and Jacques Marie Pohier. 0 8164 2169 2 120pp.

Communication in the Church. Ed. Gregory Baum and Andrew Greeley. 0 8164 2170 6 126pp.

Liturgy and Human Passage. Ed. David Power and Luis Maldonado. 0 8164 2608 2 136pp.

Revelation and Experience. Ed. Edward Schillebeeckx and Bas van Iersel. 0 8164 2609 0 134pp.

Evangelization in the World Today. Ed. Norbert Greinacher and Alois Müller. 0 8164 2610 4 136pp.

115. Doing Theology in New Places. Ed. Jean-Pierre Jossua and Johannes Baptist Metz. 0 8164 2611 2 120pp.

116. Buddhism and Christianity. Ed. Claude Geffré and Mariasusai Dhavamony. 0 8164 2612 0 136pp.

117. The Finances of the Church. Ed. William Bassett and Peter Huizing. 0 8164 2197 8 160pp.

118. An Ecumenical Confession of Faith? Ed. Hans Küng and Jürgen Moltmann. 0 8164 2198 6 136pp.

119. Discernment of the Spirit and of Spirits. Ed. Casiano Floristán and Christian Duquoc. 0 8164 2199 4 136pp.

120. The Death Penalty and Torture. Ed. Franz Bockle and Jacques Marie Pohier. 0 8164 2200 1 136pp.

121. The Family in Crisis or in Transition. Ed. Andrew Greely. 0 567 30001 3 128pp.

122. Structures of Initiation in Crisis. Ed. Luis Maldonado and David Power. 0 567 30002 1 128pp.

123. Heaven. Ed. Bas van Iersel and Edward Schillebeeckx. 0 567 30003 X 120pp.

124. The Church and the Rights of Man. Ed. Alois Müller and Norbert Greinacher. 0 567 30004 8 140pp.

125. Christianity and the Bourgeoisie. Ed. Johannes Baptist Metz. 0 567 30005 6 144pp.

126. China as a Challenge to the Church. Ed. Claude Geffré and Joseph Spae. 0 567 30006 4 136pp.

127. The Roman Curia and the Communion of Churches. Ed. Peter Huizing and Knut Walf. 0 567 30007 2 144pp.

128. Conflicts about the Holy Spirit. Ed. Hans Küng and Jürgen Moltmann. 0 567 30008 0 144pp.

129. Models of Holiness. Ed. Christian Duquoc and Casiano Floristán. 0 567 30009 9 128pp.

130. The Dignity of the Despised of the Earth. Ed. Jacques Marie Pohier and Dietmar Mieth. 0 567 30010 2 144pp.

131. Work and Religion. Ed. Gregory Baum. 0 567 30011 0 148pp.

132. Symbol and Art in Worship. Ed. Luis Maldonado and David Power. 0 567 30012 9 136pp.

133. Right of the Community to a Priest. Ed. Edward Schillebeeckx and Johannes Baptist Metz. 0 567 30013 7 148pp.

134. Women in a Men's Church. Ed. Virgil Elizondo and Norbert Greinacher. 0 567 30014 5 144pp.

135. True and False Universality of Christianity. Ed. Claude Geffré and Jean-Pierre Jossua. 0 567 30015 3 138pp.

136. What is Religion? An Inquiry for Christian Theology. Ed. Mircea Eliade and David Tracy. 0 567 30016 1 98pp.

137. Electing our Own Bishops. Ed. Peter Huizing and Knut Walf. 0 567 30017 X 112pp.

138. Conflicting Ways of Interpreting the Bible. Ed. Hans Küng and Jürgen Moltmann. 0 567 30018 8 112pp.

139. Christian Obedience. Ed. Casiano Floristán and Christian Duquoc. 0 567 30019 6 96pp.

140. Christian Ethics and Economics: the North-South Conflict. Ed. Dietmar Mieth and Jacques Marie Pohier. 0 567 30020 X 128pp.

141. Neo-Conservatism: Social and Religious Phenomenon. Ed. Gregory Baum and John Coleman. 0 567 30021 8.

142. The Times of Celebration. Ed. David Power and Mary Collins. 0 567 30022 6.

143. God as Father. Ed. Edward Schillebeeckx and Johannes Baptist Metz. 0 567 30023 4.

144. Tensions Between the Churches of the First World and the Third World. Ed. Virgil Elizondo and Norbert Greinacher. 0 567 30024 2.

145. Nietzsche and Christianity. Ed. Claude Geffré and Jean-Pierre Jossua. 0 567 30025 0.

146. Where Does the Church Stand? Ed. Giuseppe Alberigo. 0 567 30026 9.

147. The Revised Code of Canon Law: a Missed Opportunity? Ed. Peter Huizing and Knut Walf. 0 567 30027 7.

148. Who Has the Say in the Church? Ed. Hans Küng and Jürgen Moltmann. 0 567 30028 5.

149. Francis of Assisi Today. Ed. Casiano Floristán and Christian Duquoc. 0 567 30029 3.

150. Christian Ethics: Uniformity, Universality, Pluralism. Ed. Jacques Pohier and Dietmar Mieth. 0 567 30030 7.

151. The Church and Racism. Ed. Gregory Baum and John Coleman. 0 567 30031 5.

152. Can we always celebrate the Eucharist? Ed. Mary Collins and David Power. 0 567 30032 3.

153. Jesus, Son of God? Ed. Edward Schillebeeckx and Johannes-Baptist Metz. 0 567 30033 1.

154. Religion and Churches in Eastern Europe. Ed. Virgil Elizondo and Norbert Greinacher. 0 567 30034 X.

155. 'The Human', Criterion of Christian Existence? Ed. Claude Geffré and Jean-Pierre Jossua. 0 567 30035 8.

156. The Challenge of Psychology to Faith. Ed. Steven Kepnes (Guest Editor) and David Tracy. 0 567 30036 6.

157. May Church Ministers be Politicians? Ed. Peter Huizing and Knut Walf. 0 567 30037 4.

158. The Right to Dissent. Ed. Hans Küng and Jürgen Moltmann. 0 567 30038 2.

159. Learning to Pray. Ed. Casiano Floristán and Christian Duquoc. 0 567 30039 0.

160. Unemployment and the Right to Work. Ed. Dietmar Mieth and Jacques Pohier. 0 567 30040 4.

All back issues are still in print and available for sale. Orders should be sent to the publishers,

T. & T. CLARK LIMITED

36 George Street, Edinburgh EH2 2LQ, Scotland

LIBRARY OF ADDISON COLLEGE